Godfathers

Inside Northern Ireland's Drugs Ra et

Jim McDowell

Gill & Macmillan

Gill & Macmillan Ltd
Hume Avenue, Park West, Dublin 12
with associated companies throughout the world
www.gillmacmillan.ie
© Jim McDowell 2001
0 7171 3298 6
Print origination by Carole Lynch
Printed by Omnia Books Ltd, Glasgow

All photographs reproduced in this book have been
supplied from *Sunday World* archives.

This book is typeset in Goudy 10.5 on 14.5pt.

*The paper used in this book comes from the wood pulp of
managed forests. For every tree felled, at least one tree
is planted, thereby renewing natural resources.*

A CIP catalogue record for this book is available
from the British Library.

1 3 5 4 2

Dedicated to the memory of

Martin O'Hagan
1950–2001

murdered by cowards

Contents

Prologue

❦

All books should, of course, have a beginning and an end.

This one is different. It starts where it should have ended.

At the end of the book there is a chapter written by me where I say I could get shot dead for what is carried in this book, and the investigative reporting which is the hallmark of the work we all do in the *Sunday World* newspaper, North and South of the border.

That chapter was written earlier this year. And, before the book was published, someone, a reporter — an investigative reporter — was shot dead.

The victim of a cowardly bunch of shoot-in-the-back bastards masquerading as a drugs-pushing cartel under the guise of the so-called Loyalist Volunteer Force was, of course, Martin O'Hagan.

The fifty-one-year-old father of three lovely daughters was gunned down just yards from his front door as he dandered home with his wife Marie from a couple of happy hours in the pub on the Black Friday night of 28 September 2001.

It is a night now etched in infamy. Martin was the first journalist to be murdered in the thirty-two-year history of the Ulster 'Troubles'.

Five years earlier, Veronica Guerin, also fearless in her pursuit of drugs 'Godfathers', was gunned down in her car outside Dublin.

But Marty was the first reporter, hack, journalist — call all of us what you will — to be cut down in cold blood by a terrorist killer gang in Northern Ireland.

At the time of writing this, the police were still hunting Marty's murderers.

His family — wife Marie, daughters Tina, twenty-seven, Cara, twenty-four, and little Niamh, just fifteen — were struggling to come to terms with the loss of a loving husband and doting father.

Writing this nine days after Martin's despicable murder — and as tributes and condemnation and messages of condolence were still pouring into Marie's home and into the *Sunday World* offices in both Belfast and Dublin — my emotions are still a twisted tapestry of sadness, compassion, and anger.

When I think about the drugs 'Godfather' scumbags who carried out the murder, I get barbed wire in my blood.

But, in a democratic society, the decent people have to leave it to the law — and those agencies whose duty is to enforce the law — to take its, and their, course.

That is why, although we printed a front page in the *Sunday World* a week following Marty's murder that we know the killers, we could not print their names in the paper — and I, at this stage, cannot reveal them here.

The law must take its course: and if I were to name them before, hopefully, they are apprehended and brought to court, their lawyers would no doubt argue that they would not get a fair trial.

That would be the last thing that I, the staff of *Sunday World* — and Marty — want, or would have wanted.

As it is, we await justice taking its course.

And as it is, it was Martin O'Hagan, a good lad, and a loving husband, who lost his life in pursuit of the 'Godfathers' who peddle drugs — and try to poison our kids.

So it is, as a mark of respect to Martin's memory — and as a lasting tribute to his wife and family — that I dedicate this book to Martin O'Hagan: born on 23 June 1950, and who was brutally murdered by cowards on the night of Friday, 28 September 2001 … and who died a hero in doing so, bravely shielding his wife with his body as four bullets tore into his side and back.

The *Sunday World* staff — to whom this Prologue, and my thanks — were originally meant to be directed, both understand this and support it.

To them, and to my own family, thanks for all your help with this book, and your continuing, unwilting and courageous support throughout the dark days after Marty's murder.

You have pledged to carry on in the spirit of his, and your own, work.

For that, for the record, I salute the memory of Martin O'Hagan.

I salute you all.

And, in spite of the gunmen, and murderers, and 'Godfathers' — we're not bate yet!

Jim McDowell
Monday, 8 October 2001

1

Mickey 'Money Bags' Mooney — The Beginning

'Mickey, you're wanted on the phone ...'

Those six words, in the Belfast vernacular, spelt death for Ulster's first drugs 'Godfather'. And they were to spark a new twist to the terror war that has tortured all of Ireland for thirty-one years. They were the signal that the Provos were now opening up a new war front — against drugs dealers beginning to infiltrate Northern Ireland. The paramilitaries, both republican and loyalist, had always kept the lid on drugs in Ulster. After all, both sides portrayed themselves as 'protectors of the people'. But then the drugs epidemic that had hit the South, festering in such ghettos as Dublin's infamous Ballymun estate, began to seep across the border. There was too big a 'killing' to be made financially, for big-time crooks in Ulster to ignore.

And Mickey Mooney was certainly a big-time criminal. He was a 'hard man' from Belfast's Catholic/republican enclave of Lenadoon, a bleak housing estate in the shadow of the Black Mountain. He came off the hard streets of Belfast, polishing his skills in punching power by becoming a boyhood amateur boxing champion. Says one boxer trainer of him, 'He was a diamond-hard kid. He had fists of stone. He would take on anybody, in the ring or out of it. And that followed him into his later life.'

That later life was a life of crime — thieving, armed robberies, any scam going. A top policeman who had charted Mooney's 'career' said of him: 'He was expert at spotting the main chance in crime. Everything from bootlegging illegal poteen to "fencing" (acting as the go-between) to get rid of stolen or black-market goods.'

Eventually, Mooney spotted what he considered to be the biggest and best main chance of all — drugs. Not hard drugs. Not, in those early days, narcotics like heroin, but the so-called 'soft' drugs — hash, cannabis, Ecstasy tablets. However, in grabbing that 'main chance', he also wrote his own epitaph. He knew he was flying in the face of the Provos' then anti-drugs stance. (That stance was later to change.) But the 'hard man' in him didn't give a flying phoenix. He was more interested in the ash dropping off a cannabis joint — as long as he supplied it — than the Provos' maxim of a phoenix rising from the ashes.

One particular incident illustrates why. When he started his drugs operation, there was opposition of another kind — from the owners of pubs and clubs in Belfast, his main operating base. The proprietors started hiring bouncers, or doormen, to stop the drugs getting in. The most popular pubbing and clubbing area in Belfast was the city's so-called 'Golden Mile', which stretches from just outside the world-famous Europa Hotel in Great Victoria Street up into the nightclub mecca of Bradbury Place near the town's Queen's University. Bouncers, in their black ties and tuxedos, were on the doors of almost every pub.

On this particular Friday night, the 'Golden Mile' was teeming with revellers. Before he went out, Mooney put on an overcoat.

He had already cut out the right-hand pocket. He put his hand through it, and from the table in front of him he lifted a 'frightener' that he had bought the day before for £500. It was a snub-nosed, Israeli Uzi submachine gun — an assassin's 'best friend', as it was dubbed by the security forces worldwide. Mooney lifted the weapon, and headed for the Golden Mile.

Most of the bouncers knew him and treated him with respect: they knew his penchant for using his fists, and to what devastating effect he could use them. The first pair of bouncers were outside a pub. They spotted Mooney coming towards them.

'There was a certain swagger about him. There was always a threat that hovered around him,' one recalled: 'But as he walked up to us, he was smiling.'

'How's it going, Mickey?' the bouncer says he asked, although he admits, 'Even the sight of him usually made my arse sweat and my heart almost stop. He could mean trouble ...'

He recalls what happened next: 'Mooney just flapped open his overcoat. Underneath, in his hand, was the Uzi. He smiled as he waved it, discreetly, at both of us. And he simply said: "You lads know my business. Here's the deal: don't interfere with my business and I won't interfere with yours! And tell the rest of your mates inside that as well." '

Other bouncers recall how the 'calling card' visit with the Uzi was carried on right down the Golden Mile that night. 'He just didn't give a fiddler's,' said one bouncer who was visited by Mooney. 'He knew if he was spotted by the cops he could get off-side. And if there was a shoot-out ... his attitude to the law was the same as his attitude to the Provos: "F*** them." '

It was an attitude that eventually cost Mooney the ultimate price. The Provos were about to commit their first murder using the cover name 'DAAD' — for Direct Action Against Drugs.

The terrorist they chose to lead up this 'hit' team (DAAD was later to claim at least another dozen lives, all of them drugs dealers) came from another Catholic enclave, much like the one Mooney had grown up in: Short Strand, on the banks of the River Lagan in inner East Belfast, just a ten-minute stroll from the city centre. The DAAD chief was a proven, veteran bomber and gunman. And it was he who decided to lead by sinister example. He chose another seasoned IRA man from Short Strand as his second 'hitman'.

They sent out 'scouts' to chart Mooney's every move, especially when he was 'relaxing' in his favourite pub, 'The 18 Steps', which was in the busy pedestrianised shopping precinct of Ann Street, smack dab in the centre of Belfast, just a quarter mile from the City Hall. The pub was so-named because it was upstairs, on the first floor above a 'Pound-stretcher' shop. Mooney and his cohorts picked it not only because they liked it, but because anyone coming to get any of them would have to come through only one door and — they thought — they would have time to react. If Mooney was carrying the Uzi, he could open fire front-on at any would-be assassin.

But on that Friday night, 29 April 1995, the DAAD squad had another plan. Mobile phones, now the trademark and main tool of drugs dealers worldwide, were in their infancy then. But the Provo 'hit team' had at least one. They watched from another Ann Street bar as Mooney arrived and climbed up the steep stairs into the aptly named 18 Steps. He was with another man. The DAAD assassins gave Mooney, then thirty-four years of age, time to make, and take, a few phone calls. Father-of-four Mooney also had a mobile phone at that stage, but he was used to making calls on that, and taking calls on the payphone. Mobile phone calls were easily scanned in those days: landline calls weren't.

The payphone in the 18 Steps bar was at the top of the stairs. The Provos knew that. They also knew that anyone using it would be standing with their back to the stairs, and wouldn't see who was coming from behind. So the third member of the Provo hit squad stayed in the bar across the street, while the other two crossed the street. He phoned the 18 Steps number from his watching eyrie in the other pub. (There are those who say it was a woman who phoned Mooney on the payphone: that is not the information from our sources.) The payphone rang at the top of the stairs. Someone, not Mooney, answered it. 'Mickey, you're wanted on the phone,' that person beckoned.

They were the last words Mickey Mooney was to hear on this earth. He went to the phone and picked up the receiver. His two killers, not even wearing trademark balaclavas, stormed up the stairs. They were firing into the ex-boxing champ's back even before he could turn round and face them and try to put his stone-hard fists to use. He was dead before he hit the ground, a pool of his own blood swirling around his bullet-riddled body.

The gunmen merely turned round and ran back down the stairs. They had vanished up one of the small alleyways that traverse downtown Belfast before police or soldiers could even set off in pursuit. The third DAAD hit squad member merely tucked his mobile phone into his pocket, finished his pint in the pub across the street, and walked out ... to mingle among the Friday night revellers already piling into Belfast city centre. None of the three-man hit squad has ever been convicted of Mickey Mooney's murder.

There was another man with Mooney in the 18 Steps that night. After the shooting, he fled ... in fear. That same fear has kept his mouth shut ever since.

But the brutal killing didn't stop Mooney's drugs-dealing legacy from mushrooming. The first 'Godfather' was dead, but his legacy was a growing Mafia of others, eager to step into his blood-stained shoes. When Mooney had been in prison, serving terms as a so-called 'ODC' — Ordinary Decent Criminal, as opposed to terrorist or gangster (or drugs 'Godfather') — he had handpicked members of his own gang for when he got back out from behind bars. He wanted a team of 'enforcers', men like himself, bred, born and 'buttered', as they say in Belfast, in the teak-tough backstreets of his native city. He found them in the prison exercise yard in the shape of similar 'hard men' like Edmund 'Big Edd' McCoy.

McCoy had built a growing, and glowing, reputation as a street fighter: a bare-knuckle prize fighter with a hair-trigger temper. Like Mooney, he didn't look it. He wasn't a muscle-bound, weight-lifting replica of Arnold Schwarzenegger. He was, like Mooney, all bone and sinew — and searingly fast and effective with his fists.

On one occasion, he and another hard man had staged a bare-knuckle prize fight in the dead of night, lit up by car headlights, in the middle of the huge car park at the Marks & Spencer superstore at the massive Sprucefield shopping centre on the outskirts of the garrison town of Lisburn. The 'man-to-man dig', as they call it in Ulster, was watched by scores of spectators: gangs of both McCoy's and the other hardman's supporters. And although it was an illegal event — bare-knuckle prize-fighting is outlawed in the UK and Northern Ireland — thousands of pounds in bets changed hands. Eyewitnesses say the fight lasted just two minutes and McCoy won easily.

After Mickey Mooney's death, McCoy 'graduated' to become a drugs 'Godfather', taking up where Mooney had left off. He too was to be gunned down, also by the Provos, in a Belfast bar. 'Big Edd' McCoy's short life and hard-man times are chronicled in Chapter 15.

But he wasn't the only legacy Mickey Mooney left. There was also Mooney's brother, roly-poly twenty-two-stone Liam 'Fat Boy' Mooney. After Mickey's death, 'Fat Boy' (or 'Bargain Bucket' as he is also known because of his penchant for Kentucky Fried Chicken bargain buckets — several pieces of chicken and several portions of chips) moved into drugs dealing, big time, and in more ways than one. But his lumbering bulk wasn't all soft tissue. He could be hard-headed when it came to making money from drugs, although there were other elements of his life where he wasn't so street-smart, or smart at all.

He followed my car one night. I managed to shake him off and get my car parked. I stood outside the pub where I was to meet a contact, and waited for my pursuer to inevitably turn up. The drugs dealer eventually drew up with his driver. He was a cheeky bastard, leaning out of the car window to give me abuse, but, characteristically for him, not taking up my invitation to get out of the car. He sneered: 'I suppose you are here to meet one of your f*****g contacts.'

I told him I was, and to look behind him. I informed him that my contact was sitting in the car right behind his. When he looked round, he took off like a bat out of hell. For sitting behind him was Superintendent Kevin Sheehy, then head of the RUC Drugs Squad.

When Liam Mooney teamed up with cohorts to build his gang, smuggling in drugs from the Republic, Liverpool, Amsterdam and Spain, he went for the 'heavies' — ex-paramilitaries with a sinister past and a menacing future. One of those was, and is, Kevin 'Maxi' McAlorum. He wears flash leather waistcoats, tight jeans and big-buckled belts. And with his shoulder-length hair and Zapata-style moustache, he looks like a dope-smoking hippy. He's anything but. And he, too, almost paid with his life for drugs dealing. But it wasn't DAAD this time. It was an organisation he'd allegedly once belonged to, the Irish National Liberation Army (INLA), who tried to kill him as he sat with his nine-year-old daughter, Barbara, in a house at Ashfield Gardens in the terror-ridden 'Murder Triangle' of North Belfast. Gunmen fired through the front living room window of the house at 9 p.m. on the night of 14 March 1996.

'Maxi' McAlorum lived. His young daughter, sitting on his knee, died in a hail of gunfire. She was said to be the 'voice and ears' of her deaf-and-dumb mother. Her father said of her killers: 'She was an innocent child. They are nothing but cowards, complete scum.' The picture of the innocent little primary schoolgirl lying in her coffin was published extensively afterwards.

The killers were later linked to terrorist Hugh 'Cueball' Torney, who was in the thick of one of many INLA feuds at the time. Later, McAlorum was to say: 'I heard it was the INLA and if it was, then I am mystified because I have never had any dealings with that organisation.' At the same time, he claimed he was on an IRA death list for 'antisocial behaviour'. (The Provos were claiming he was involved in drugs.) And the RUC had raided his home just weeks before the fatal shooting, seizing £1,600 during what they described as a probe into 'serious crime'.

But while the bullets meant for Liam Mooney had cut McAlorum's young daughter's innocent life tragically short, it did not deter him from his drugs-dealing interests. Just a few weeks later my colleague Hugh Jordan and I were on our way to Dublin to 'doorstep' — confront and take pictures of a cross-border drugs dealer in the Southern capital. We took a phone call on the road: if we detoured to Dublin airport immediately, we were reliably informed, we would get pictures of 'Fat Boy' and his lieutenant 'Maxi' coming off a plane from Amsterdam.

Mooney was known to go shopping often in the Dutch drugs mecca, carrying up to £30,000 in cash in plastic supermarket bags (another name he had in the drugs trade was 'Money Bags', a nickname that his elder, by now deceased, brother also had appended to him by some in the drugs racket). On his continental shopping list were cannabis and E tabs.

We confronted Mooney and McAlorum. Mooney warned me not to take his picture as I leaned over the barrier at the arrival gate. I kept on taking pictures with a small camera. Mooney didn't know that 'planted' further up in the arrivals hall was our photographer Conor McCaughley with a zoom lens, banging off every movement.

As McAlorum pranced around like a demented ballet dancer, Mooney ominously warned: 'Don't be putting our pictures in your paper' (the *Sunday World*). I asked him if that was a threat. There were uniformed Garda Síochána nearby. If he was threatening us, I'd have got him arrested. He huffed and puffed, and eventually pushed his airport trolley, laden with presents for his kids and duty-free cigarettes and booze, away to the car park. The toys from Amsterdam were for now. The drugs would be shipped in later.

A few months later, early on Thursday morning, 3 December 1998, two DAAD gunmen called at Mooney's heavily fortified house at Carryduff, in a middle-class suburb six miles from the centre of Belfast. They had hijacked a cable TV company van. When Mooney's wife opened the door at around the time she would have been taking the kids to school, the bogus cable TV 'engineers' stopped her to ask for a bucket of water. When she turned round to oblige, they shoved her to the ground and barged past her. They foraged through the house, guns in hand, looking for 'Fat Boy'. Luckily for him, he wasn't in. He was in

Amsterdam, buying more drugs. Otherwise, he would have gone the same way as his brother. Now, Mooney is on the run in Spain, wanted by police in Dublin after jumping bail on drugs charges.

But the killer organisation, DAAD, is still on the rampage, in spite of the IRA ceasefire. They operate under a no-claim, no-blame basis — they don't admit their catalogue of killings, so they can't be blamed. But, as they say in Belfast, the dogs in the street know who the murder gangs really are.

As for Mickey Mooney, their first assassination target, he never knew who his killers were. He had his back turned, on the payphone. And he wasn't to live to know that his death in blood-stained shoes was the first in a DAAD killing spree against a dragoon of other drugs dealers.

The Sequel

Blood-stained shoes … That last sentence in the first part of the Mooney saga was prophetic.

The first part of this chapter was written before 11 April 2001. But late on that date, a chilly Wednesday night in early spring, a young lad wearing blood-stained shoes lay writhing in agony. That night, Michael Mooney Junior, the son of Ulster's first drugs 'Godfather' and aged just twenty, was 'four-timed'. He was shot in both kneecaps and both ankles, and was left with blood running down his legs and feet, soaking his blood-stained shoes. Just as his father had been, Michael Junior appeared to be the victim of Provo gunmen.

At first, police said that he had been kidnapped by a gang of masked men in Vara Drive in West Belfast on the night in question. According to their sources, he was given a 'severe hiding'. Next, they said, he was taken to an alleyway off Beechmount

Grove in the Falls area of West Belfast, where he was shot in both ankles and both knees. He also suffered severe facial injuries.

But initially, the police got it wrong. Vara Drive, where at first they said Michael Mooney was abducted, is in a loyalist area at the top of Belfast's Shankill Road. Drugs dealers often cross the 'peace lines' between republican and loyalist areas, particularly in Belfast. It is undoubtedly dangerous, but it is how they do business.

Any suggestion — from whatever source — that Michael Mooney may have been in a loyalist area would therefore have given the impression that he was, like his late father, dealing in drugs. However, there was no evidence to substantiate any such claim.

When the story of his shooting appeared on the front page of the *Sunday World*, four days after it occurred, Michael's mother, Mickey Mooney's widow, Anne, phoned me. She wanted the whereabouts of his kidnap clarified, insisting that he had in fact been picked up in a nationalist area off the Springfield Road in Belfast, that he was not anywhere near the Shankill on the night he was shot. She insisted, forcefully, that her wounded son, who was by that stage in a 'stable' condition in hospital, was *not* a drugs dealer.

She also said that, as with her late husband, she believed that the Provos had shot Michael Junior.

The story of Michael Junior's shooting appeared on the front page of the *Sunday World* on 15 April. The headline ran: 'PROVOS SHOOT DRUG LORD'S SON.' Anne Mooney, in spite of all we had written and published about her murdered husband, phoned me on the following Tuesday. Surprisingly, there was no 'aggro', just a reasoned conversation.

By the following Thursday, the police had clarified where Michael Mooney had been picked up. Anne Mooney had said it was in Forest Street in a nationalist area, not in a loyalist district as at first put out by the police and that's how it turned out to be.

This is her story, which appeared in the paper on Sunday 22 April:

The widow of murdered drugs 'Godfather' Mickey Mooney has told *Sunday World*: 'My son is no drugs dealer.'

Anne Mooney was speaking after our front-page story last Sunday revealing that her son, Michael, twenty, had been shot by the Provos during the previous week.

He was kidnapped by masked men, beaten, and shot in both knees and both ankles in an entry off the Falls Road in Belfast.

He was at first said by police to have been picked up by a gang in the Woodvale area of Belfast.

That worried Mrs Mooney. She insisted her son wasn't kidnapped in Vara Drive, as at first reported.

And the residents of the small street in the Woodvale were insistent during the week that no such incident had occurred there.

However, Mrs Mooney contacted the police herself.

And it was later revealed that Michael Jnr had been picked up in a street on the nationalist side of the Springfield Road, and not in the loyalist area as first reported.

We were eventually told he was kidnapped from Forest Street, before being taken to an alleyway in the Beechmount area of the Falls and 'four-timed' — shot twice in both the knees and the ankles.

First reports also said Michael Mooney Jnr had suffered serious head wounds in a beating, as well.

But Mrs Mooney told us midweek that her son was 'recovering well'.

However, when asked if her son was shot because he was a drugs dealer, she replied: 'No, he is not a drugs dealer.'

Asked who she believed had shot him, she said: 'Who did you say in the paper?'

When told we pointed the finger at the Provos, she said: 'I believe that too. It was them.'

Asked to comment on rumours that her son had recently been involved in a row with IRA men in the Short Strand area of Belfast, she replied: 'That's not true, either. He wasn't involved in any row there.'

Asked why, then, her son had been targeted for the shooting, she said:

'That wee lad has been persecuted and victimised since he was fifteen.'

Asked why, Anne Mooney said: 'Because of his name.'

That was an obvious reference to Michael Jnr's father, Mickey Mooney.

He was Belfast's first drugs 'Godfather'.

He was also shot by the Provos. But he died at the scene of the shooting in a downtown Belfast bar in late April 1995.

He was an ex-champion boxer who could, as they say on the streets, 'handle himself'.

And because of the way the father-of-four dressed — he was thirty-five when he was assassinated — he was known in the city's underworld as 'The Dapper Don'.

So there you have it: a savage sequel being visited on the son of Ulster's first drugs 'Godfather', who also suffered a savage shooting.

Mickey Mooney died. His son, Michael Junior, lived. But for Anne Mooney, the wife of the former, the mother of the latter, it must have been heartbreaking to have first a husband, and then a son, lying shot ... both in pairs of their own blood-stained shoes.

2

'DAAD's Army'

'The war's almost over — let's go to war.'

In one simple, cold-blooded quote the Provisional IRA's strategy for an all-out assault on drugs dealers is summed up. Throughout the thirty-one years of the dirty, brutal sectarian war euphemistically called 'the Troubles', the Provisional IRA first of all set themselves up as the 'Protectors of the People'. That was in the early days when the hardliners broke away from the Official IRA, because there wasn't enough iron will, there weren't enough weapons to protect Catholics — like those living on the lower Falls Road on the interface with the Protestant and loyalist Shankill in West Belfast — from the burning-out pogroms of fire-in-the-belly Protestants and the flying bullets of the B Specials, once an RUC part-time militia, since disbanded.

So the Provos broke away. And the Provisional IRA mantra ever since has been that the organisation and its volunteers are the 'Protectors of the People', a propaganda ploy that is still used to this day. As such, the PIRA set its face against drugs dealers — as did the loyalist paramilitaries for most of the thirty-one-year terror war. The summary justice meted out to traffickers, rubberstamped by so-called 'kangaroo courts', was swift and primitive — kneecappings, beatings, expulsions, deadlines giving small-time drugs dealers twenty-four hours to get out of the country. One Sinn Féin activist even earned the nickname 'White Socks'; when his kneecapping victims, many of them teenagers, were lying face-down in alleyways on their bellies to be shot through the back of the knees, he stood at their heads, and, as their heads craned up in pure terror, the last thing they saw before the bullets tore into their flesh, ligaments and bones was ... his white socks. In those days, to dabble in drugs was deemed to constitute 'antisocial behaviour'. But, in the early days, and throughout much of the Troubles, there wasn't much drugs dealing around.

Meanwhile, the Provisional IRA, from their original chrysalis as merely 'Protectors of the People', had grown into something much bigger: a killing, shooting and bombing terror machine that was no long reactive, but pro-active. They quickly built up arsenals and brigades, not only to rebut Protestant or police incursions — they believed they could take on both — but also the British government, which ran the 'Occupied Six Counties of the North of Ireland'. Their goal was that which republicans for generations had hankered after, and fought and died for: a united Ireland. The history of that 'struggle', now abandoned for a more political process with ex-terrorists and former representatives of terror sitting in the devolved Assembly at Stormont, contesting and being elected to Westminster seats, and targeting Dáil Éireann in Dublin for more political power, doesn't need to be repeated here. It is amply documented elsewhere. But what does need to be illustrated in the context of this book is how the Provos needed to switch tactics to retain their mantle as the 'Protectors of the People'.

They did that through a two-pronged strategy. The first was a sustained black propaganda campaign aimed at discrediting the 'Black Bastards', the RUC. The fruits of that were borne out by the eventual establishment of the Commission chaired by Chris Patten, the former British Tory Governor of Hong Kong. Patten, a former professional footballer and junior minister at the Northern Ireland Office in Belfast when Britain operated a policy of Direct Rule in the Province, had overseen the handover of Hong Kong to the Chinese. He was later called in by Tony Blair's Labour government to head up a Commission which held a sustained series of consultations with all sections of the community in Ulster, and come up with a blueprint for 'reforming' the RUC. This he did. That wasn't good enough for the Provos. Their demand had been 'Disband the RUC'. They didn't get it all. Instead, they got a new police service for Northern Ireland. At the time of writing, they were still agitating for more radical 'reform', even though the RUC was being decapitated by the number of very senior officers — men who had devoted a lifetime to protecting their community by putting both republican *and* loyalist terrorists behind bars — taking the 'Patten Package' (an early retirement deal intended to create space for more Catholics to join the new service.) Many of those getting out were leaving angered, embittered, and in disgust. But while all of this was happening, the Provos had made the RUC *personae non grata* in great swathes of republican/nationalist housing estates and districts throughout Northern Ireland.

So in came the second strategy. The Provos set themselves up as 'Protectors of the People' for a second time. And this time, the tactic was to 'police' their own areas. If people were mugged, raped, assaulted or had their homes burgled or broken into, they were not to turn to the police for 'justice' — they were to turn to the Provos. The only reason they were to involve the police at all was merely to report the crime, so that when their homes were burgled, for instance, they could claim their losses back from insurance companies who required a formal police or RUC report. But as for summary justice and punishment — the Provos became the 'People's Police'. So-called 'punishment beatings' and shootings spiralled.

And as drugs took hold in the South of Ireland, in the now heroin-ravaged estates like Ballymun in Dublin city, so 'soft' or 'recreational' drugs began to take a hold in the North of the island. What had started as a trickle of E tabs and 'blow', or cannabis, with the likes of Mickey Mooney, soon became a flood. Parents were scared: afraid for their teenage sons and daughters. Afraid that estates like Ballymurphy, in the Provo heartland of West Belfast, could become another Ballymun.

Simultaneously, the Provos were winding down their 'Long War' against the Brits and the Northern Ireland 'Statelet', as they dubbed it, to graduate to the next stage of their 'struggle'. They once had infamously boasted of 'the Armalite in one hand and the ballot box in the other'. Now, the deadly assault rifle was to be abandoned, or at least put out of use. The next assault was to be on the ballot box.

And one main plank in a party policy of winning hearts and minds to get the votes for Sinn Féin was simple. Pick on the new breed of criminals who had, already, the blackest of names: the drugs dealers. And go to war on them. That would win the overwhelming support of the people in the street. 'Everyone hates drugs dealers,' the Provo strategists reckoned, 'so let's hammer them'.

And so, another small, cell-structured, compact killing machine was born — DAAD. Direct Action Against Drugs.

Instead of the Irish Republican Army, there would be DAAD's Army. It was to consist of a ruthless band of hardened, veteran terrorists.

Most Northern drugs dealers, in those days, operated in Belfast. So DAAD's base was established in the Short Strand district, a redeveloped housing estate of brown-brick houses nestling on the banks of the River Lagan, and, importantly, less than a mile from Belfast City Hall, smack dab in the centre of the city. DAAD were to learn to keep their operations tight. As in Mickey Mooney's murder, just a close-knit team of at most three 'hitmen' operated with military-style planning and precision. But the idea behind DAAD, of striking at drugs dealers — especially if they had links to rival republican groups like the INLA and the IPLO — was blueprinted by the IRA itself, before it declared its first ceasefire late in 1994, and before it needed a front organisation like DAAD to kill on a 'no claim, no blame' basis.

One such occasion was the so-called 'Night of the Long Knives' in Belfast on 25 April 1994. On that night, car convoys of armed Provos fanned out across the city, under the noses of patrolling armed police and soldiers. Drugs were only beginning to take hold then. Mickey Mooney was emerging as the first, and still the only, 'Godfather' at the time.

But sixteen men were 'kneecapped' — shot through the leg. Others were badly beaten — battered with baseball bats and hurling sticks: brutal, bone-crushing weapons in themselves, even more so with six-inch nails driven into them to puncture skin and skulls. Others were ordered out of the country in the Provo mini-pogrom.

And one man — Francis 'Rico' Rice, a Catholic — paid the ultimate price for pushing drugs. He was shot dead. The body of 'Rico' Rice, twenty-three, was discovered the morning after the

'Night of the Long Knives' at a place called Half Moon Lake in Lenadoon, West Belfast, just a quarter of a mile from where he lived with his girlfriend. He'd been shot five times in the head ... after first escaping an IRA gang who burst into his home (he jumped through a first-floor window), and then being told by the waiting gang when he phoned home later to check that his fiancée was all right, that it would be OK to return and meet them.

IRA sources said later that the Provo sweep would have resulted in more deaths if they had been able to find their intended murder victims. In all, they claim, up to one hundred homes were visited that night. And it was then that the IRA let the cat out of the bag about their future role as 'Protectors of the People' if the Long War waged since 1969 was indeed to wane — as it did, temporarily, with the ceasefire being announced five months later, on 31 August 1994. An IRA statement said of the purge against drugs users and small-time pushers: 'We are not waging war on the community. We are supporting the community in the war against drugs.' The statement added that they were 'not just taking people out and shooting them'. The Provos said: 'We have directed some people to youth clubs and substance-abuse centres. We have told the parents of others.' All of which was a bit late for twenty-three-year-old 'Rico' Rice.

The purge against drugs pushers crystallised the new, evolving role of the 'protectors of the people'. After the IRA ceasefire in the autumn of 1994, the Provos could no longer be seen to be directly involved in such killings. Instead, the murder mantle was taken up by DAAD. DAAD's Army was mobilised. Big time. And its march was to continue right through a litany of life-taking and 'punishment' operations. Mickey Mooney, who died almost a year to the day after 'Rico' Rice's killing, may have been the first drugs 'Godfather' to end up dead at the hands, and trigger fingers, of DAAD. He wouldn't be the last.

Other 'Godfathers' of Ulster's burgeoning drugs empire were to follow: 'Speedy' Fegan, Brendan Campbell, 'Big Edd' McCoy, and up to a dozen lower-profile dealers and runners, like Paul 'Saul' Devine, gunned down in a street opposite the City Hospital in Belfast on 8 December 1995. Just out of prison four months after being jailed·for handling stolen goods, he had been a 'runner' for Mickey Mooney. When his boss was gunned down the previous April, Devine, a thirty-five-year-old Catholic, had placed a sympathy notice for Mooney in the death columns of the Belfast morning paper, the *Irish News*. In doing so, he may have signed his own death warrant. One of the trio of DAAD assassins who shot him six times in the back before putting a single bullet in his head as he lay on the ground was believed to be a woman. They all wore woolly hats. No one has been caught, charged or convicted of the crime.

Some of the higher profile 'executions' carried out by DAAD are documented in this book. And DAAD is still operating today, except that the 'old hands' have stepped back into the shadows, and the 'New Guns in Town' have taken over (see Chapter 16).

And so it was that drugs, and the drugs 'Godfathers', provided the Provos with the targets they needed to re-mould their role as self-styled 'Protectors of the People', and to move from one war-footing to another, through the pseudonym 'DAAD'.

As the Provos and Sinn Féin dipped their toes into the democratic process as the next stage of their struggle for Irish independence, this image/role fitted the bill. Disband the police on the one hand. We'll be the 'People's Police' on the other. And if that means drugs dealers dead on the street … well, we can't be blamed, we can't be kicked out of the democratic process. We didn't claim it. We can't be blamed for it. But, with a nod and a wink, 'our people' know what the score is.

Most people, though, were revolted by both the killings and the cynicism of the killers.

3

Billy 'King Rat' Wright

'This is a message from the Commanding Officer of the Mid-Ulster Brigade of the UVF. The message is simple. He is placing you, the *Sunday World* staff, the people who produce the *Sunday World*, those who advertise in it, those who deliver it, and those shopkeepers who sell it under the threat of death. There will be no further warnings. To live, you must cease publication immediately.'

The place was an office on the first floor of a building close to Woodvale Park at the top of the Shankill Road in Belfast. The recipient of the blanket death threat was me, Jim McDowell. I was trying to run the *Sunday World* bureau in Belfast at the time, after the same UVF Commander had tried to torch that office with a crude firebomb: explosives packed around a drum of petrol. The bombers had ordered the staff in the office at the time out at gunpoint. Two of the most senior staff, Northern Editor Jim Campbell, shot previously on his own doorstep by the UVF, and veteran reporter Martin O'Hagan, later tragically murdered, had to get out of Northern Ireland at that period, for their own safety.

I was running the Ulster Press Agency, a freelance agency, with another reporter, Joe Oliver. The *Sunday World* people came to see me. They asked for support and assistance to stop a paramilitary terror gang from shutting a newspaper office, and perhaps silencing the Ulster edition of the *Sunday World* — which has two almost distinct editions, North and South. The response was that the Ulster Press Agency moved into the *Sunday World* office, which had survived the bombing attempt because the detonator on the firebomb was faulty. The newspaper office, and its Belfast-based staff and freelances, continued to function. If the bullyboys using bombs and bullets had stopped them, where would it end? Which newspaper would be next? Where did that leave freedom of speech, freedom of expression, and freedom of the Press? Buckling then would have been a victory for fascism.

For a while, that faction of the UVF — extreme even by that organisation's standards — seemed satisfied with the flight of the two senior journalists from the Belfast office. But the 'truce' wasn't to last long. It wasn't too long afterwards when an intermediary from the UVF on the Shankill Road contacted me. He said that a meeting had been set up for the next day. He said it would be vital to the interests of the *Sunday World*, and everyone who worked for it in Belfast, that I should attend. I told him I couldn't fit in the meeting for the next morning. He said there could be no change. I knew something serious was afoot.

When I got to the meeting my misgivings were confirmed. The overall Commanding Officer of the UVF in Ulster was there, a pipe-smoking, middle-aged man. As it turned out, it was not he who wanted to see me. But in the end, his presence, and his later mediating role, proved both crucial and valuable. I was told someone was arriving from Portadown. I knew immediately who to expect: Billy Wright, aka 'King Rat', the CO of the Mid-Ulster

Brigade of the UVF, and the terrorist who, we believed, had ordered the bomb to be placed at gunpoint in the *Sunday World* bureau on the top floor of offices in Belfast's busy High Street, just beside the city's famous Albert Clock.

He came in, oozing menace, with his 'minder', a terrorist-turned-drugs dealer still active at the top of the Loyalist Volunteer Force. He and Wright had been the targets of a series of IRA assassination plots. Wright was spartan in appearance. His hair was tight-cut, almost shaven. He was built like a superbly fit middleweight boxer. And it was he who, in cool, calculated and measured tones, spelt out the blanket death threat, almost leaning on every syllable 'on behalf of the CO of the UVF's Mid-Ulster Brigade'.

Of course, everyone in the bright, airy room that day, drinking cups of tea, knew who the CO of the Mid-Ulster Brigade was. He was Billy Wright, the quasi-religious loyalist zealot who was doing the talking. Wright always talked about himself in the third person. It was a technique that almost drove anti-terrorist detectives crazy on the many times he was lifted and taken to the interrogation centres at either Gough Barracks in Armagh or the Castlereagh holding centre in East Belfast. There, terrorist suspects could be held and questioned for seven days before either being charged or released. Wright used to claim that he was arrested and detained so many times — especially when, in that old cliché, Ulster was 'on the brink' of 'plunging over the abyss' — that it amounted to a personal form of internment for him. When held in those centres and asked about a litany of terrorist atrocities, he would stonewall by telling shifts of questioning detectives: 'Billy Wright wasn't there' or 'Billy Wright didn't do that' or 'Billy Wright didn't order that', and on and on and on ... always in the third person.

Everyone of an age to think and analyse in Northern Ireland — and beyond in the Republic — knew that Billy Wright *was* the CO of the UVF in Mid-Ulster. And so it was when he issued the blanket death threat against the *Sunday World* and everyone he deemed to be associated with it. But, of course, he was only delivering it on behalf of the 'CO of the Mid-Ulster Brigade'.

It would be stupid to say anyone faced with such a threat wasn't concerned, or afraid. I was — not just for myself, but for everyone connected with the newspaper, and their families as well. Wright was ruthless. When he was eventually shot dead inside the Maze prison just after Christmas 1998, security forces reckoned that he had been directly, or indirectly, responsible for forty-seven deaths, many of them the murders of innocent Catholics, most of them in County Armagh's infamous 'Murder Triangle'. If the IRA carried out an atrocity, Wright would not only try to match it, but outdo it.

His philosophy, explained to me that afternoon in that office, was simple: retaliate with such vengeance against IRA or any other kind of republican atrocities, and the message would get home to the Provos: 'it's your own people who will end up hurting most.' I found out much about King Rat that afternoon. I sat with him, face-to-face across that table, for over two hours. I countered his 'philosophy' on issuing death threats and killing people for ideological objectives — the same as I did with Hugh 'Cueball' Torney of the INLA. But Wright was having none of it. He charted, articulately and in detail, the making of this man that lots of people thought was a monster, a psychopathic killing machine. He talked about the people close to him, members of his family, murdered or left maimed by republican fanatics. At one stage, he invited me to put on my coat and accompany him out onto the nearby Shankill Road. He said that if he told people out on the Road that I was from the *Sunday World*, I would be 'kicked to death'.

I had to tell him that he was from Craigavon, and that the people in the room, as well as quite a few people on the Shankill, politicians and community workers among them, already knew me. And that I had helped put together the community newspaper, the *Shankill News*, for years: doing the design and layout, and chaperoning it through the printers — in Craigavon, his own backyard, incidentally — for nothing. Just to help the community. And always to hammer out the message of peace, and 'Stop the Killing'.

'Stop the Killing' was a maxim close to my heart. It was the slogan we adopted when myself and a PR man named Alan Moneypenny (later to work on a major project on the Shankill) called a meeting of newspaper editors in Belfast. We wanted the newspapers — especially the Unionist *News Letter* and the Nationalist *Irish News*, both morning dailes — to join a campaign to promote a huge peace phone-in called, simply, 'Stop the Killing'. The British Telecom chief PR man in Belfast, Frank Johnston, swung in behind us. A peace rally was to be staged outside Belfast City Hall with Irish Congress of Trade Unions chief Peter Cassells coming up from Dublin as one of the main speakers. We held the phone-in over the twenty-four hour period spanning the day of the rally. Northern Ireland has a population of just under one and half million people. No less than 528,000 people — men, women, children, OAPs — phoned in. They demanded one thing: 'Stop the Killing'. The public had had enough. More than enough of the slaughter of the innocents.

But that message wasn't getting through to terrorist 'Godfathers' like Billy Wright. Not at that stage, anyway. That was to come later with the joint ceasefires of 1994. And the folk who organised that massive peace phone-in were told later that, at least, the result had influenced republican long-term strategists like Gerry Adams, the Sinn Féin president. But Wright was a closed book.

During the course of that marathon confrontation with him, he told me a story that left me cold, and suggested collusion between some elements of the security forces and loyalist paramilitaries. There has been plenty of evidence — and propaganda — in the past about such liaisons. But confirmation came when I asked Wright why an active service unit of the Mid-Ulster Brigade of the UVF had shot dead a mother of five who was seven months pregnant. She was Mrs Kathleen O'Hagan, thirty-eight, from Creggan in County Tyrone. Wright first of all denied he did it. 'Billy Wright didn't do that,' he said, again using the third person. Did he order it? 'Billy Wright didn't order it,' he replied. So who did it?

Billy Wright answered by telling a story. Eight Protestant workmen had been blown up by a massive IRA landmine as their van passed Teebane Crossroads in County Tyrone. The 'crime' the building workers had committed was to work in an army base: the IRA had murdered people for 'aiding and abetting the Crown forces of occupation' many times before.

It was one of the worst atrocities of the Troubles. I reported Teebane that night. It was the night before the Ireland v. Wales rugby match in Dublin. The then Secretary of State for Northern Ireland, Peter 'Babbling' Brooke, was in Dublin for the game. He appeared on the Gay Byrne 'Late, Late Show' on Friday night. He knew about the Teebane tragedy by then. And he was still suckered into singing 'My Darling Clementine', as policemen and policewomen were calling at homes to tell the weeping and wailing relatives of the Teebane dead about what had happened to their menfolk. There was, rightly, an outcry about Brooke's behaviour.

I had tickets for the Lansdowne Road match the next day and late in the evening drove on down to Dublin with my wife. But as we walked towards the ground on the Saturday, we just couldn't stomach the idea of going to a thriving, thrashing, singing, chanting rugby game ... as the bodies of those men were being put into coffins to be taken home to their families. We stopped a couple of Welsh supporters who were coming back from the ground after refusing to pay what the touts were asking for tickets. We gave them ours. Later we went for a walk in Dublin, to Trinity College, to look at the Book of Kells — a revered Christian book in what, after the occurrences of the previous night at a County Tyrone crossroads, seemed still a pagan country.

Anyway, Wright had an allegation to make about the pregnant woman. He claimed that someone she knew was on the end of the command wire that detonated the huge landmine bomb at Teebane. Wright said the bomber was up the hill above the crossroads, with a Provo accomplice. He claimed that the woman, who eventually died cowering in a corner trying to protect her unborn child, was in a public telephone box a quarter of a mile from the crossroads on the Friday night of the landmine atrocity. Wright claimed that as the workmen's van passed the telephone box, the woman in the callbox phoned a cellphone number. The cellphone was being held by one of the two bombers on the hill. Wright claimed that the woman signed the workers' death warrants when she told one of the two-man bomb team: 'That van's just passed ...' The bombers on the hill had only seconds to wait. The van hit the crossroads. And the huge blast from the massive landmine hidden at the side of the road wiped out the lives of eight good men going home with their pay-packets to their wives and families on a Friday night after a hard week's labour.

But Wright said the terrorists who murdered the woman hadn't only gone looking for her. They had been tipped off that one of the hilltop bomb team would be in the house that night, too. He wasn't. The woman was shot dead, anyway. I said that what he told me still didn't justify the killing of another human being, especially a woman, and especially a mother with another unborn baby in her womb. Wright just looked at me. He didn't flinch.

But it was that kind of ice-cold killer instinct for which Billy Wright eventually paid with his life. He had become a true 'Godfather' — of Ulster's dirty, vicious, sectarian war. Later, he was to be kicked out of the UVF, and sentenced to death himself by that organisation, after becoming a 'Godfather' of another kind — in the drugs trade. As for that blanket death threat on the *Sunday World* and people associated with it, it was the CO of the UVF in Ulster overall who played a crucial part in having it lifted. I met with Wright again the following morning in the UVF's Shankill Road HQ. As he walked down the skinny corridor in front of me to the office in the inner sanctum, a politician from the Progressive Unionist Party, the UVF's political wing, who was walking in the opposite direction, grabbed me by the arm and said: 'McDowell, what are you doing with that mad bastard?' Wright heard him, but didn't react. I knew then we were out of trouble. Inside the office, after more talking, the overall CO said the blanket death sentence would be lifted forthwith.

I don't know what he said to Wright when I left. But there was no more hassle from that quarter — until Wright was 'stood down' by the UVF general command. Plus, the UVF was becoming worried about his 'pathological' love for killing, and ordering people to be killed. He had also built his own, ultra-loyal power base in Portadown. And he could have tried to stage a coup, at any stage, to try to overthrow the ageing overall UVF command in Ulster, based on the Shankill Road headquarters known as 'The Eagle'. When I had asked Wright during our first 'death threat' meeting how he thought his life would end, he pointed out the window towards the Shankill Road. He said his coffin would be carried up there, with the Ulster flag and his black gloves and beret on top. After the UVF in effect expelled Wright — under threat of a death sentence himself — Wright knew that was not to be.

When Billy 'King Rat' Wright was 'stood down' by the UVF as their 'commander' in mid-Ulster, and told to flee the country or face death — with another ex-UVF man — Wright defied the parent organisation.

He went to ground in Portadown. And he set up the alternative terror gang, the Loyalist Volunteer Force. He also took the maxim of his former UVF mid-Ulster Brigade with him: the title of the Tina Turner rock hit — 'Simply the Best'. He proudly wore polo shirts with the motto on his left breast, above his heart.

But the LVF under Wright were to continue to carry out some of the worst and most heartless atrocities in the history of the Troubles.

And the LVF got into drugs, to finance their terror operations — and their penchant for luxury homes and alloy-wheeled 'Beamers' (BMWs) and other fast, and luxury, cars. That was one of the reasons Wright was kicked out of the UVF. They reckoned that while still Commander of their Mid-Ulster Brigade, he was personally pocketing £2,000 a week from the drugs sales at one County Down nightclub alone.

Indeed, in his role as a drugs-dealing 'Godfather', as well as a terrorist one, there were claims that he dealt in drugs with a notorious ex-INLA man based in the Cathedral town of Downpatrick, County Down. It was also alleged that this ex-INLA man was dealing in drugs and other criminal activities with the crime king known as 'The General' in Dublin. The General was Martin Cahill. 'Was', because he, too, died at the point of an assassin's gun in broad daylight, in the Irish capital city, which was his favourite stomping ground.

But if Wright was also dealing with The General indirectly, through the Downpatrick go-between, it wouldn't have been the first time The General had linked up with loyalist terrorists from Portadown, where Wright based himself and lived. Security forces believe that The General masterminded the theft of the multi-million cache known as the Beit Paintings from a stately home in the South of Ireland — and then 'fenced' them through loyalist terrorists in the North (the UVF in Portadown were pinpointed, and that's the organisation Wright started in and then became CO of its Mid-Ulster Brigade). The IRA never liked The General for that. They believed that the Northern loyalists used the money from the Beit paintings deal to buy guns to kill Catholics. Also, it was reported that the Provos, keen to expand their financial empire, were muscling in on some activities of the Dublin underworld — where INLA gangs were heavily into the drugs-dealing scene, too. So it came as little surprise when Martin 'The General' Cahill was gunned down in Dublin. And that the IRA got the blame.

Wright's chain of drugs-dealing conduits certainly stretched further than the North. The main lines of supply into Ulster were from the South and it was known that the go-betweens — the 'Fixers', like Paddy Farrell (see Chapter 5) — were dealing with the kind of Dublin criminal crews who were later to order the murder of Dublin crime reporter Veronica Guerin. The

'Fixers' brought the big consignments of drugs in. It was after they were split that the loyalist paramilitary 'Godfathers' went for the pickings, and then sold them on to their 'runners' and the young people prepared to pay for them.

As is still the case today, there were those in paramilitary gangs who said they were prepared to fight, and die, for the 'honour' of their country: but when it comes down to it, there is no honour among drugs dealers of any hue, or, as the plethora of killings on the streets of Ulster has proven, among drugs 'Godfathers' either.

In April 1997 Billy Wright was finally convicted on charges of threatening to kill a woman. He was being held in the 'H-Blocks' at the Maze, in the Loyalist Volunteer Force wing. He had been sentenced to eight years in jail. Typically, like all the other times he had been questioned by police about his role as 'Godfather of terrorism', he pleaded innocence. When charged with intimidating the woman and her son — they fled the country after the trial — he replied: 'With all my heart and with total honesty, I am innocent of both charges and genuinely believe they are sinister and political.' The judge in the case took no such view. Instead he described a still defiant Wright as 'a sinister man'.

The LVF prison wing, with Billy Wright as CO, occupied one side of an H-Block. The INLA wing was in another. And inside the INLA wing there was a republican terrorist as ruthless and committed as Billy 'King Rat' Wright. He was Christopher 'Crip' McWilliams, and he planned to murder Billy Wright.

McWilliams was serving a life sentence for the cold-blooded murder of bar manager Colm Mahon at the door of a Belfast pub. Again, it was drugs. Colm, a good man known to reporters who frequented the bar where he was manager, had told drugs dealers to get out. They told him they would be back in ten minutes to shoot him. Rather than let any of his staff stand at the door, he stood there himself. The 'team' barred from the pub were known members of the Irish People's Liberation Organisation (McWilliams was later to join the INLA). On that fateful night for Colm Mahon, 5 December 1991, two of the gang returned to the doors of the bar ten minutes after their threat had been made. And one of them shot Colm Mahon, point-blank, in the face. The punters inside the bar were having a pre-Christmas party as Colm — a slightly built thirty-nine-year-old father of three whose family had already suffered tragically in the Troubles — died instantly from a single bullet wound to the head as he stood by the door.

'Crip' McWilliams got life for that murder. He is now out of prison under the early release terms of the Good Friday Agreement (despite the Wright killing). He still denies it was he who fired the gun. He says he was 'fitted up' for that crime by the police.

But it was McWilliams who 'fitted up' Billy Wright for murder in the Maze jail. His murder plan was simple. With two of his INLA cohorts, the trio would worm their way out of their compound and cut a hole in the security fence at the front of the shared H-Block. They had handguns smuggled in. They also got their hands on wire clippers. The yard in front was where the bus picked up prisoners to go to the visiting centre — separately, of course. Just as there was segregation of loyalist and republican prisoners on the 'Blocks', so, too, there had to be at visiting times. But McWilliams had learned that Billy Wright was having a visit on the Saturday morning after Christmas Day of that Christmas week in 1997.

The big question still remains: How did McWilliams *know* Billy Wright's movements? One theory is that it was standard practice for the names of prisoners going to receive visits to be called out over the jail tannoy system. But Wright's father is still pursuing an 'official conspiracy' theory, alleging it was a government or secret service plot to have his son assassinated.

On that Saturday morning, when the prison van came to pick up Billy Wright, McWilliams and his two co-assassins, having cut their way out of their compound after clambering over its roof, pounced on the van. Billy Wright was in the back. He was unarmed, of course. McWilliams wasn't. And McWilliams shot him dead. There were rumours later that Wright pleaded for his life. McWilliams later denied that. He said that Wright had 'come at' him, and would have grappled with him if he, McWilliams, had not, as he put it, 'put him down'.

The prosecuting brief at the trial of the INLA trio told the court: 'This was a daring operation depending on split second timing. It was carried out in broad daylight with no attempt to cover up what they were doing or their identities. It was clear Mr Wright was under no illusion as to their intentions of his possible fate. He was seen to kick out at his attackers but was shot several times and succumbed rapidly from the injuries sustained.'

There was also a claim from inside the prison afterwards that McWilliams laughed as he sprinted back to his cell. He later denied that, claiming he 'didn't derive any sense of malicious satisfaction from being party to the demise of a fellow human being'.

A siege in the INLA wing of the jail threatened immediately after the shooting as armed police and troops were called in. It was sidestepped when a priest was summoned. The assassins handed over two guns, a 9mm Makarov pistol and a double-barrelled .22 Derringer, to the clergyman before giving themselves up. The 'job' was done. McWilliams and his cohorts became immediate heroes among hard-bitten republicans.

Although McWilliams got life for the murder of Billy Wright, he was released less than *two years* afterwards, under the terms of the Good Friday Agreement.

Earlier this year, McWilliams was reported to be suffering from cancer. He was also, reportedly, getting ready to run in elections for the Irish Republican Socialist Party, the political wing of the INLA. However, if the cancer doesn't kill him, there are still plenty of other loyalist terrorists who want to, especially among the LVF, still active in Portadown. Some of the LVF's members are still in jail — in Maghaberry jail now, as the Maze has closed down.

The murder of Wright inside the Maze threatened to blow the whole peace process apart. Many times down through the years of the Troubles, politicians and churchmen had warned that Ulster was 'teetering on the edge of the abyss', that a 'Doomsday scenario' plunging Northern Ireland into civil war was imminent. In the wake of the Wright killing, a wave of violence did erupt in loyalist areas. The LVF murdered a number of Catholics.

However, in the days, and weeks, after Billy Wright's murder, two factors mitigated against mass murder on the streets. The UVF had expelled Wright. And their death threat had been carried out — not for them, but without them having to do it themselves. So the UVF kept the lid on their 'teams'. And the Ulster Freedom Fighters (UFF), at that stage, had no formal links with the LVF. So they weren't going to move, either.

As for who 'set up' Billy Wright inside the jail ... well, the UVF had waged a black propaganda war against him since booting him out of their ranks. They claimed he was a puppet of the British secret service agency MI5, known to be involved in a 'dirty tricks' campaign in Ulster. Others pointed the finger elsewhere.

Billy Wright's father and family still believe there was a cover-up over the entire circumstances of his murder. They are still demanding a public inquiry.

4

Hugh 'Cueball' Torney

'Let me make it clear. If another story appears in the *Sunday World* about the INLA being involved in drugs dealing, it will not be you who will be shot. It will be one of your reporters. The reporter will be shot through the side of the head, not the front, so that it is a slow death — like George Seawright. And then it will be you who will bear the responsibility of telling their family who shot them, and why the reporter died.'

The terrorist doing the talking was Hugh 'Cueball' Torney, originally from West Belfast, but who lived most of his life on the run — from both the security forces, who, at that time, wanted him for about seven murders, and from other factions within the Irish National Liberation Army, because he had either shot at, or shot them, during bitter internecine republican feuds.

Nevertheless, at the time he was making this threat, he was back in his native Belfast. In a pub, at a meeting with me. I had agreed to Torney's request for a meeting, so that I could tell him that I, and the people who worked with me, didn't agree with any organisation, be it loyalist or republican, taking lives in pursuit of ideological goals — or, for that matter, delving into the then only burgeoning, but potentially very lucrative, drugs-dealing racket. I had arranged to meet 'Cueball' and his colleague — who, like Torney, was subsequently murdered by 'his own' — in a public place in the heart of Belfast, just in case. But Torney, being hunted by both the RUC and Garda Síochána on both sides of the border, wasn't exactly prepared to meet in front of the City Hall. Instead, he chose an alleyway, a cross between a back entry and a side-street, which runs between a well-known pub and what they call in Belfast slang a 'cream cookie's': a bookies, a betting shop. In Belfast, there is always a flow of people between a public bar and a bookmaker's betting shop: the relationship between swigging pints and punting on racehorses has always been close and intimate. So if Torney, or his co-terrorist, were going to do anything — well, at least there would be witnesses, if the cops ever caught up with them.

However, Torney was standing outside the betting shop on his own wearing a leather jacket, with a bulge in the left-hand side. It didn't take a Mensa IQ to work out what was in there, and it wasn't a big, generous and compassionate heart. The greeting was cool, and cautious. My colleague, Hugh Jordan, was caught up on another story at the time, but he had arranged to meet us later, in the upstairs lounge of a pub I had already specified.

When I got to Torney, he asked me to wait a minute. He said the guy with him was in the bookie's, 'doing a bet'. But before his accomplice came out, someone else emerged from the bookie's. He was a senior Unionist. Someone who the INLA would have loved to shoot at that stage. He was known to like a bet. He was also known to like a wee tipple, a gin and tonic, during the day.

As soon as Torney spotted him, his eyes lit up. His hand started moving towards the open zip of his leather jacket towards where the lump was on the left-hand side. And I told him: 'You can't do that. Not here. Not to him. He's unarmed. And, anyway, if you shoot him here, there's myself and most of the punters who have just walked by us into the bookie's as witnesses.' Torney looked at the Unionist as he came towards us. He looked at me. He said: 'Then I'll just have to blow you — and any of them who come out — away as well.'

But just then the senior Unionist came walking towards us. He came right up. And he said to me: 'Jim, I've a story for you. I need to talk to you.' I said: 'Not now. Away for a pint in that pub down there, and I'll see you in half an hour ...' The sweat was beginning to bubble on my brow. I thought: this Torney I am standing eyeball-to-eyeball with is a madman, a megalomaniac, a psychopathic killer ...

But Torney suddenly just looked at me. He looked at the politician. He pulled his hand out of the inside of the leather jacket. His mate had just walked out of the betting shop. And he said: 'Come on — where are we going to talk?' The senior Unionist went for his pint. However, his lucky escape was only part of the story.

I went with Torney and his cohort to the bar Hugh Jordan and I had already specified. Torney went in front up the stairs to the first-floor lounge. As we walked up the carpeted steps, I pretended to stumble. I knocked into the back of his legs. He stumbled and grabbed the wooden bannister. At least his finger-prints are on that, I thought. If he shoots me, there will be some forensic evidence. Torney just turned round and smirked. 'Nice try,' he said. 'But if I have to shoot you — no one will be in any doubt who did.'

At the top of the stairs, in the lounge bar/restaurant, where they served crocodile steaks and ostrich meat — yes, even in those days in a tired Belfast torn asunder by the Troubles, Hugh Jordan was waiting at the bar. Torney and his mate were not impressed with that level of privacy — or the lack of it. We went to a 'snug', a private benched-off area, where we could have our own table. There was no offer of a meal. Torney and his cohort sipped only orange juice. Torney immediately got stuck in.

The *Sunday World* had been running a series of stories about the local people on the New Lodge Road in North Belfast beginning to baulk and buck at the increasing drugs assault on their kids. They had even organised themselves into a group producing pamphlets and leaflets not only highlighting the growing problem, but warning against it — and pointing the f inger at the INLA. Torney, making no bones about it, wanted to impose himself, and his organisation, as self-appointed censors of the newspaper.

And that's where the Hugh 'Cueball' Torney threat against one of our reporters came in — with foreshadows of the callous killing of drugs-racket probing Dublin crime reporter Veronica Guerin later to follow.

He said he wouldn't shoot me, or Jordan, but would 'take out' a reporter and shoot that person in the side of the head so the reporter would die slowly — like George Seawright, a firebrand loyalist politician whom the INLA had previously assassinated.

It was the turn of both myself and Hugh Jordan to baulk and buck at what amounted to a bare-faced death threat. We felt like going for the guy. But he had the gun.

Torney knew 'the odds'. And suddenly, he just stood up, stared, drained his glass of orange juice, and walked out of the upstairs snug in the lounge bar, without even a backwards glance.

His threat was never to come to pass. A bullet — a number of bullets — in his back were later to stop Torney's bully-boy tactics and end his reign not only as an apologist for drugs running, but as one of the most ruthless 'Godfathers' of terror in the history of the Troubles.

On 3 September 1996 he was shot dead in the tinderbox town of Lurgan, County Armagh, by 'his own', as part of another vicious internal vendetta. Ironically, the 'crime' that finally earned Torney the death sentence from his former associates was, of all things, declaring a ceasefire. In April 1995, Torney and three others were arrested by the Garda Síochána at Balbriggan, on the road back to Belfast from Dublin. Anti-terror detectives, who had been tipped off, sparked a snatch operation in which four rifles, two machine-guns, twenty handguns and 2,500 rounds of ammunition were seized. Torney's response, as the then leader of the INLA faction, was to try to buy time — and buy his freedom. He instructed his lawyer to announce at the first court hearing that the terror gang had called a ceasefire. That was enough to get him out on bail. And to allow him to return to a role he knew well — that of fugitive. He busted the bail conditions and went on the run.

But the 'hawks' in INLA ranks back in Belfast interpreted that as treason to their cause. They believed that 'Cueball' had prostituted their so-called 'terms of engagement' to slither out from behind bars. It was made known in republican circles that Torney had been deposed as 'chief of staff' and replaced by another ruthless killer and 'revolutionary', Gino Gallagher. But Torney's rejected 'rump' faction believed that Gallagher — once close to Torney — was going to shoot 'Cueball'. So instead, in broad daylight, at 11 a.m. on New Year's Eve, 1995, they murdered thirty-two-year-old Gino Gallagher as he sat in what is known in Belfast as 'the broo' — a social security bureau — halfway up the Falls Road in the city.

Gallagher had just sat down at a client cubicle window when his killer, wearing a wig — a favourite disguise of Torney's —

stepped up behind him and shot him repeatedly in the back of the head. 'Cueball', in spite of his marathon terrorist past, was just forty-one years of age.

It wasn't long before Torney's turn came. He was walking along Victoria Street in Lurgan with another man. The pair were ambushed. Torney was shot from behind, bullets peppering his back. But he still managed to spin around. Bullets flew. Torney tumbled, to die in a pool of his own blood only seconds later. It was like a scene from the Wild West. Rescuers who rushed to his aid turned him over. Underneath his body they found a Beretta 9mm gun. Strapped to his waist they found a holster.

As in the past, faced with death, Hugh Torney was no stranger to gun law. He had been in gun fights with the British army, with the Official IRA, and, resulting from feuds, up to his neck in vendettas within the INLA. His first brush with the British army was way back in 1970, when he narrowly missed being shot dead. He was also on a loyalist UVF hit list. They accused him of masterminding an audacious and daring triple murder in which one of their commanders, Colin Craig, was cut down in a hail of bullets, right in the heart of Belfast's ultra-loyalist Shankill Road. That was in June 1994. In 1987, he escaped assassination in a double killing that sparked yet another INLA feud, and led to yet another republican split when the Irish People's Liberation Army (IPLO) was set up. That hair's breadth Houdini act happened in the Rosnaree Hotel outside Drogheda, on the main Dublin–Belfast road. Thomas 'Ta' Power and John O'Reilly, both high-rollers in the INLA GHQ faction, were drinking tea with Torney. Gunmen wearing false beards burst in. They shot dead Power and O'Reilly. Torney was wounded, but survived. The attack was said to have been ordered by another INLA faction-fighter, Gerard 'Dr Death' Steenson (who was later to die by the bullet as well, another victim of what were then serial INLA internal feuds).

And to give just a fleeting insight into the bloodletting of those vendettas, Torney had been jailed in the early 1980s on the word of an INLA 'Supergrass' at an anti-terrorist (no jury) trial in Belfast. There were twenty-seven accused in the case, later to be released on appeal. A quarter of those were later killed — all but one shot dead by former 'comrades-in-arms'. Torney, Jimmy Brown, John O'Reilly and 'Ta' Power, Henry McNamee, Michael Kearney and Gerard 'Dr Death' Steenson. An eighth INLA man involved in that 'Supergrass' trial was Martin 'Rook' O'Prey, stalked and shot dead by loyalist gunmen after being linked to a series of assassinations.

As for the claims from the people of the New Lodge Road that the INLA were up to their oxters (armpits) in drugs at that time, there was one other interesting drugs angle. RUC sources have linked Gino Gallagher to the murder of drugs dealer Paul 'Saul' Devine close to the Russell Court Hotel complex in Belfast a month before he, himself, was shot dead. However, that killing was claimed by DAAD, the Provo 'front' gang. It was suspected at the time that Gallagher was being threatened by the Provos. And to save his own life, the theory goes, Gallagher did a deal with DAAD — to 'take out' Saul Devine. If that was the case, he was acting for the Provos and not the INLA.

Gallagher was 'lifted' by the police and questioned about the Devine murder. He was released without charge. They knew that Gino was no stranger to the gun: he, too, had been linked to the triple murder of three top UVF men on the Shankill Road in Belfast, as well as the killing of anti-drugs pub 'bouncer' Jack Smyth, gunned down where Gallagher had allegedly struck before — at the door of a pub/restaurant on the ground floor of what had been the old Russell Court Hotel on Belfast's Lisburn Road.

As for 'Cueball' Torney's accomplice that day in Belfast when he issued the shooting threat against a reporter, he sat mute and silent throughout the whole episode, and was impeccably dressed — even wearing a Queen's University graduate's scarf. He was John Fennell, a founder member of the INLA, from the city's fiercely republican Ardoyne district. He was later bludgeoned to death with breeze blocks after being kidnapped and interrogated. His battered and bloody corpse was found on 4 March 1996 at a caravan park in Bundoran, County Donegal. He was forty years of age when he died. He had vamoosed from his native Belfast shortly after the murder of Gino Gallagher. The Garda Síochána detectives probing Fennell's demise believe he was another victim of the seemingly interminable INLA feuds. He was still a member of the GHQ Staff faction headed up by Torney.

Belfast Councillor George Seawright was shot and fatally wounded as he sat in a taxi at Dundee Street, off the Protestant Shankill Road, in mid November 1987. Both the INLA and their split offshoot, the Irish People's Liberation Army, had been looking for him. They branded him 'outrageous' and a 'bigot' because, among other things, he called for revenge when loyalist paramilitaries were murdered. But what put him top of their 'hit list' eventually was his statement at a meeting of the Belfast Education and Library Board in Belfast, where he was one of the City Council's nominees, that the best solution for Catholics and their priests was that they should all be 'incinerated'.

There was later confusion about the identity of the gunman who shot Seawright. The names of two extreme republicans, both veteran INLA men, were in the frame. Both had known, run with, and operated with Hugh 'Cueball' Torney and the INLA faction in the past. They were Jimmy Brown and Martin 'Rook' O'Prey. The mystery of Seawright's murderer has never been solved: both Brown and O'Prey later fell prey to the gun in Ulster politics themselves.

But George Seawright took a long time to die. He was shot and seriously wounded in mid November 1987. His life-support machine was switched off on 3 December. The thirty-six-year-old loyalist firebrand — he was a Scot who had moved to Belfast to live and marry — regained consciousness at one stage in the Royal Victoria Hospital in Belfast. He couldn't speak, and could hardly see, because of the brain damage he'd suffered by being shot 'just' in the side of the head. But he managed to write down a name for his wife alleging who had set him up for assassination. The name he wrote down for his wife Liz, later to take his place on Belfast City Council, was that of Jimmy Craig. Craig was a top officer in the loyalist Ulster Defence Association (UDA), and was known as a hardman and a gangster. He ran protection and other extortion rackets throughout Belfast. And he had also colluded with the INLA when it suited both organisations to get money. That was before the drugs revolution struck Belfast and Northern Ireland and before the INLA became involved in the drugs racket. But George Seawright suspected, knew even, that Craig was colluding with the INLA even then. And his deathbed message was simple — Craig had also colluded in his shooting, with whichever gunman had fatally wounded him.

The Ulster Freedom Fighters, who are closely allied with the UDA, later carried out an official investigation into the activities of Craig under the guidance of their then leader John McMichael. George Seawright's murder didn't feature prominently within that compass. Instead, the McMichael-ordered probe embraced claims of other criminal, and profit-making, collusion between loyalist and republican paramilitaries, including the INLA and the IRA. It also investigated how a one-time commander of the Ulster Volunteer Force (UVF), separate from the UDA, but also a loyalist terror organisation, was gunned down by the Provisional IRA. The Provos had taken a van into the heartland of loyalist West Belfast to the street where the UVF commander lived. They opened fire on him out of the back of the van when they swung open the back doors, not far from their quarry's own front door. Their victim was the infamous Lenny Murphy, a butcher, whose stock-in-trade was leading a bunch of crazed loyalists who picked up innocent Catholics in taxis, or off the streets, and used butchers' knives to torture, mutilate and murder them. They were called the Shankill Butchers. Craig was also accused in loyalist terror circles of colluding with the IRA to set up Lenny Murphy.

It was against that bloody backdrop that Jimmy Craig, whose stomping ground was the Shankill area of West Belfast, was ulti-mately lured to the Castle Inn bar (now called the Bunch of Grapes) in the heart of another UDA/UFF stronghold, Ballymacarrett, in East Belfast. He was gunned down as he stood at the bar on the night of Saturday, 15 October 1988, just under a year after the Seawright shooting. He died in a pool of his own blood. The Ulster Freedom Fighters — the then 'young bloods' taking over from the former UDA 'Godfathers' — claimed the internal killing.

In their statement, the UFF said Craig, then aged forty-seven and a father of five, was 'executed for treason'. They alleged he had also set up John McMichael himself for murder, this time by an IRA booby-trap car bomb. McMichael was trying to steer his organisation towards politics. He had also ordered an internal probe into UDA topliners lining their own pockets from racketeering and gangsterism. Craig was a prime suspect in those murky waters.

5

Paddy 'The Fixer' Farrell

'You're mad if you think that Paddy Farrell would ever have allowed himself to be tied up. She didn't murder him. It was made to look like that. And then she was blasted with the shotgun. To make it look like she had committed suicide.'

Indeed, on that day, when one of the biggest Irish drugs dealers of all time, known as 'The Fixer', was found tied to a bed in a house in Drogheda, stone cold dead, with the mutilated blonde head of his mistress resting close by, that is exactly what it looked like. Paddy Farrell, a multi-millionaire who criss-crossed the border to stitch up huge drugs deals with the likes of Martin Cahill, the Dublin gang boss known as 'The General', was married, but having a torrid affair with a stunning blonde, much younger than his wife. Her name was Lorraine Farrell, but she was no relation to 'the Fixer'. It was said that using the cover of a top-of-the-range car sales business, he could 'fix' almost anything.

And then, after the dramatic discovery of his body in that Drogheda house on 10 September 1997, it seemed that his peeved and angry mistress Lorraine Farrell had 'fixed' him. For good. The story was that Farrell, an insignificant-looking individual who dressed in sober suits, was lured into a kinky sex session by Lorraine. As the story went, she tied him to the bed, after stripping off most of his clothes. But instead of giving him the 'blow job' he anticipated, she produced a 12-bore shotgun. And as Farrell lay writhing, sweating and trying to get out of the wrist shackles with which his sex-siren mistress had tenderly and lovingly trussed him to the bed-head, she blasted his life away. And then she turned the gun on herself and blew her own brains out. The gun was found beside her body.

The motive behind Lorraine's actions was said to be simple. She had found out Farrell was going to dump her. He had made his millions. He didn't want to end up dead on a mortician's marble slab like a growing band of drugs barons. And he was planning to start a new life in America. Whether with or without his own wife has never been revealed. But Lorraine Farrell had found out there was no place for her in the plans for the flit across the Atlantic. And a woman spurned and scorned in love ...

However, truth be told, no one was ever arrested or charged for the brain-splattering murder of Paddy Farrell. That was put down to the lovely Lorraine. Well, it was convenient, wasn't it? A bit messy given the gore in the bedroom, perhaps. But a clean-cut case if it was taken at face value. And the world, and Ireland, was rid of another senior drugs 'Godfather'.

The problem is, people in the evil drugs trade don't believe that. I'll tell you why. Just a few months ago, a major player in the drugs scene approached the *Sunday World*. He knew all about Paddy Farrell's luxury lifestyle. He knew how he laundered the money from his huge drugs transactions by going across to England, buying top-of-the-range Mercedes cars, for cash, and bringing them back to Newry to sell them North and South of the border. It meant his drugs earnings were 'cleaned' instantly.

No cheques, no traces, just straight cash for cars bought across the Irish Sea, bring them back home, and flog off the five-star vehicles to whoever wanted them. The drugs dealer who approached us also knew that Paddy Farrell liked living high on the hog. Maybe not back home, for appearance purposes. Living too flash a lifestyle in Ireland would attract too much attention, not least from the Drugs Squads operating in the RUC, the Garda Síochána, and the Customs and Excise services based in Dublin and Belfast. No, Paddy Farrell liked exotic holidays. Places where he could indulge his love of fine wine and women, and rub shoulders with other gangsters. The Florida Keys, Las Vegas, the Cayman Islands, the Bahamas. He was known to be a bit tight with money and preferred, according to close associates, to lavish it on himself, not others. Which is where the exotic holidays come in.

The major player on the drugs scene who approached us had pictures of another drugs 'Godfather' at play on a Caribbean island —jet-skiing, power-boating, water-skiing, night-clubbing, swilling champagne, smoking big, fat cigars. Lazing in the hot, noon-day sun on sparkling white, wave-lapped beaches. He was Edmund 'Big Edd' McCoy. He too was to die at the point of a Provo gun, and it was after his demise that we were approached with the pictures of the Caribbean holiday he featured in. We published them to illustrate the luxury lifestyle pursued by these evil men who live off the profits of poisoning our country's kids.

But the drugs big-timer who approached us also knew Paddy Farrell. Northern Ireland is not a big place: Newry is an hour's fast drive away from Belfast, and another hour from Dublin. Farrell's network stretched between both capitals, and beyond. And whether he was into kinky sex with his blonde mistress or not, the drugs trade insider who came to us was adamant. His quotes are carried at the start of this chapter, but they are worth repeating.

At a meeting at a secret location — he said if he was spotted meeting us, he would get 'a wooden overcoat' (a coffin) — he told us:

'Don't believe a word of this "lovers' tiff" stuff. It was made to look like that. Both Paddy and Lorraine Farrell were murdered. But she didn't murder him. And she didn't commit suicide. Both were murdered.'

The clear implication? Paddy 'The Fixer' Farrell had tried one fix too many. There were rumours that he had rubbed up a top republican the wrong way, that he had 'stroked' a man who had made millions for the Provos through smuggling and other rackets, and who was also a renowned gun-runner. There was even a suggestion that this republican had started 'bankrolling' bigger and bigger consignments of drugs being brought into Ireland by Farrell. Farrell's drugs contact network was extensive. He didn't care who he worked with. Renegade loyalists or republicans. And the contact who supplied us with the pictures of 'Big Edd' McCoy, another drugs murder victim, had no doubt who killed Paddy Farrell, who then blasted Elaine Farrell into oblivion, and who 'fixed' the Fixer to make it look like a lover's tiff taken to extremes, and ending in jealousy-crazed murder and suicide.

For legal reasons, we can't divulge names. But, again, the trail led back to the Provos. And it was the Provos, after all, who were suspected of gunning down one of Farrell's main criminal associates, Martin 'The General' Cahill, in broad daylight, in a Dublin Street. The General's killer — or killers — have never been caught. And, insisted our drugs underworld contact: 'The killer, or killers, of Paddy Farrell and Lorraine Farrell have never been caught, either. And take it from me, it wasn't Lorraine who murdered Farrell and then committed hari-kari. It's only mugs who believe that. What happened had all the markings of a Mafia-style crime: a perfect crime. No one to blame but the victims themselves. A "laundering" operation for murder. Just as Paddy "The Fixer" Farrell ran a near-perfect laundering operation for his drugs money ...'

6

Brendan 'Bap' Campbell

❦

'We missed him the first time. We won't miss him the second. We know which ward he's in. We're going up there now to finish the job ...'

Those were the spine-chilling words phoned into the *Sunday World* office that spelt the beginning of the end for Brendan 'Bap' Campbell. The phone call came at tea-time the night after the Provos tried to murder Campbell the first time.

That was in the Three Kegs tavern on Belfast's Boucher Road in January 1998. The bar sits in splendid isolation, the only pub at the heart of a sprawling, modern industrial and enterprise zone sandwiched between the republican Falls Road and the loyalist 'Village' area off the Donegall Road in South Belfast. During the day, the Boucher Road is a beehive of commercial activity. At night, it becomes a wasteland, much like the Bog Meadows swampland that the whole industrial estate was built on. Just why Brendan Campbell chose to be in such an isolated spot was, at first, a mystery. Both he and his mate Brendan 'Speedy' Fegan — together known as the 'Terrible Twins' — loved carousing with women — and the women loved their flash lifestyles, always 'loaded', always flashing the cash — they could pull out rolls of banknotes when they were boasting in bars — and always cruising in flash cars. However, Campbell had parked his latest flash car, a brightly coloured American import, outside the Three Kegs bar on the night he was first targeted for assassination. That in itself was a signpost for the Provo 'hit team' to strike. But there was another element, which the *Sunday World* uncovered later, that ensured the gunmen knew where Campbell was. And it solved the mystery of why the big-time drugs dealer was in such an isolated, and therefore prone, place. Frankie 'Studs' Lanigan had lured him there.

Lanigan was a known 'wide boy' around Belfast. He came from the West of the city, and was always around the fringes of republican paramilitaries like the Irish National Liberation Army — one of the first terror gangs to split from the Provos — and the IPLO (the Irish People's Liberation Army). Lanigan was also known to be closely connected to terrorists involved in bloody internecine INLA and IPLO feuds, like the infamous Gerard 'Dr Death' Steenson.

Steenson and his rivals were at one stage embroiled in an internecine vendetta that saw a dozen people dead, most of them gunned down in Mafia-style 'hits', before the months-long power struggle eventually ended when the Provos stepped in and ordered it to end. Somewhere along the way of his nefarious existence, however, Lanigan got himself into the position of owing the IRA something: perhaps even his life. So he was set up by the Provos to set up Brendan Campbell.

He was with Campbell in the Three Kegs pub that night of the first assassination bid. And the deadly deal was that while Campbell was to be shot, Lanigan would be left alone. The Provos knew the pair were in there because Campbell's car was parked outside — one of only a handful of vehicles on the virtually deserted industrial estate road. And when two Provo gunmen stormed in, 'Studs' Lanigan, who had earlier scouted out the place, jumped into a stand-up fridge/cooler. So he was out of harm's way.

But Brendan Campbell wasn't. However, he had balls, and he showed it that night. As the gunmen fired bullets at him, he fired back, but only with bottles and glasses and ashtrays and anything else he could lay his hands on in the almost empty pub. And he moved quickly. Running for his life, literally. Almost body-swerving the flying bullets, and wearing his bullet-proof vest, he hit the stairs leading up to the lounge above the public bar. One gunman had emptied his magazine. Campbell was still banging bottles down the stairs at the second gunman, still in pursuit. Campbell got into the top lounge. He thought he could jump out an emergency exit door, or smash a window. But all the windows were barred on the outside, and the door was bolted and padlocked.

Campbell panicked. He was still hurling anything he could get his hands on. And he'd been hit and wounded. But he wasn't the only one to panic. So did the gunmen. Shots had been ringing out for over a minute. With the silence hanging over the Boucher Road at that time of night the cacophony of gunfire could be heard over a mile away. The gunmen could already hear police sirens. They scarpered. So did 'Studs' Lanigan.

When the police and paramedics arrived, they found Brendan Campbell shot and bleeding, but not seriously wounded. He was rushed to the Royal Victoria Hospital in Belfast, just about a mile away from the scene of the shooting in the Three Kegs tavern. A surgeon operated on him, removing two bullets. He was put in a 'secure' ward in the hospital, normally reserved for members of the security forces who had been ambushed, shot, or injured by terrorist bullets or bombs. Two plainclothes police guards were posted on the ward door, just in case.

That caution proved well founded. The next evening, the phone call came into the *Sunday World* office, with the chilling message: 'We're going up there now ...' I asked who was calling. The voice on the phone said: 'You know me, McDowell. It's Studs — Frankie.' The phone then went dead.

I knew how these people worked. We were the newspaper that was consistently highlighting the drugs problem, and profiling and naming the drugs barons. It was typical of their bravado to tip us off before they did something like this, so that they could brag 'We told you so' afterwards. But that is not how this paper works. Our policy has always been to try to prevent death and murder, not promote it. So I lifted the phone immediately and talked to a police officer I knew at Castlereagh Barracks in Belfast, the main anti-terror HQ. I told him about the phone call. Immediately, he contacted the police HQ in West Belfast, at Grosvenor Road RUC station, situated just three hundred metres from the back gate of the Royal Victoria Hospital on the Grosvenor Road.

A few minutes later, I got a phone call back. Three police Land Rover jeeps, full of heavily armed officers, had been scrambled from the station yard at the Grosvenor Road barracks. They raced to the hospital and Brendan Campbell was whisked out of there right away and taken to another hospital. But it wasn't just Campbell I was concerned about. It was the policemen guarding him in the hospital ward, as well. They could have been shot too.

However, Campbell didn't stay in his new hospital bed long. He knew that lying in hospital, wounded, he presented an easy target. So he signed himself out before the treatment was completed. He did a runner to England, fearful that the second death threat would be realised back home.

But he couldn't stay across the Irish Sea. He was a big-timer in Northern Ireland among his own compadres. And, anyway, he'd escaped another death bid before when gunmen tried to shoot him in his home, and he hadn't run away then. Plus, he would miss the gain from the drugs trade, and the glory among his own crowd. Especially now that he had escaped a murder bid by the most feared killer gang of all: the deadly DAAD organisation. That hyped up his 'macho man' status. He loved showing off his bullet wound scars to his harem of girlfriends, on whom he lavished money and 'trinkets' — gold chains, gold medallions, gold jangling bracelets, the hallmarks, literally, of the drugs trade and its acolytes. 'He was,' says one veteran police officer, 'living a mini Al Capone lifestyle: wild women, fast cars, late nights, wads of cash, dealing in drugs all night, drinking, then "kicking on" with his cronies when the legitimate bars opened next day.'

But then Brendan Campbell's own hype went to his head. He thought *he* owed the Provos one. This drugs 'Godfather' thought *he* would teach the *real* 'Godfathers' of terror, the IRA, a lesson. Campbell had used his contacts on the shady side of paramilitarism to help him and his cohorts 'tool up' with Czechoslovakian hand grenades, the same sort of grenades that jailed Michael Stone, the UFF Milltown cemetery massacre perpetrator, had tossed at an IRA funeral in a futile attempt to kill Gerry Adams and Martin McGuinness of Sinn Féin.

Campbell and a posse of his cronies got, in their terms, 'liquored up'. It was the dead of night and he and his mates drove to the Falls Road. At the top of the Falls sits Connolly House, the main Sinn Féin HQ, smack in the heart of the republican hotbed of Andersonstown. The house is named after one of the 'hero' Irish republicans of the past, James Connolly, whose efforts helped lead to the foundation of the Twenty-six-County

Republic of Ireland, or 'Free State' as it was first known. The house itself, a big, detached, heavily fortified converted dwelling is almost an icon to Sinn Féin followers. It has been attacked many times, with bullets and bombs, by loyalist terror gangs.

Now, on this night, it was Campbell and his cohorts who attacked it. They tried to lob the grenades over the fine wire-mesh fence strung outside Connolly House. But they were, in Belfast parlance, 'Brahms and Liszt' — 'pissed', drunk out of their minds. The grenades exploded harmlessly, one even missing its target altogether and slightly damaging the nameplate and door of an office *next door* to Connolly House. But the sound of the blasts wakened the folk of Andersonstown, normally alert to the crack of bullets or blast of bombs because of a litany of terror attacks and incidents in their area all down the years of the Troubles.

And Campbell and his mates had made one *big* mistake in their drunken, and ultimately ineffectual, grenade assault. They had gone to Connolly House in Campbell's car. Another flash car. Just like on the Boucher Road murder bid, it was Campbell's love of flash cars that was to put the gunmen on to him. But this time, it would be for good. They were not to miss killing him again.

It was well known that Campbell had returned to Belfast. He had the wheel of another flash car in his hands. And another pretty woman on his arm. She was with him the night he died. Again, he was living high on the hog. He was coming out of an upmarket restaurant. Since the Troubles started to subside, Belfast's Lisburn Road in the leafy South suburbs of the city had begun to prosper. It probably has the biggest selection of restaurants — Indian, Chinese, Malaysian, European, other gourmet eating houses — of any street, road or avenue in the city. It drew Campbell like a magnet. He was known to frequent those restaurants.

And so it was on 9 February 1998 that Brendan Campbell parked his usual top-of-the range white BMW car in Brooklyn Street just off the Lisburn Road. He thought he was relatively safe. But he may as well have been in Brooklyn, New York. In the bad old days of the terror war, whenever Ulster politicians dined out, they picked restaurants as close to police stations as possible, just in case of attack. They knew there was at least some deterrent factor for gunmen or bombers if they were eating out within easy observation distance of RUC officers manning security lookout post bunkers outside police barracks. So it was with Campbell. He was in a trendy restaurant, called 'Planks', opposite the huge and newly built RUC base on the Lisburn Road. But that didn't stop his assassin cutting him down just yards from the police station.

As Campbell and his girlfriend walked to their car, they were stalked by a lone gunman. As Campbell, aged thirty, and his female companion, aged just nineteen, walked to the parked and gleaming BMW, the gunman got a gleam in his eye. Campbell tried to flee. But it was third time unlucky. The 'Houdini' drugs dealer who had escaped death twice already couldn't cheat it this time. Bap was shot dead, his teenage dining companion seriously wounded. Brendan Campbell died quickly, lying in a pool of his own blood, just yards from the front of a police station.

Paradoxically, he had been seeking the protection of the police, whose Drugs Squad would have liked nothing better than to put him behind bars to shatter his status among his cronies as yet another of Ulster's growing band of drugs 'Godfathers'.

After Brendan Campbell's demise, I was in a bar on Belfast's Golden Mile one Saturday night.

The *Sunday World* had consistently named Campbell and his buddy Speedy Fegan as big-time drugs dealers. Yet, never enough evidence was collated, it seems, to put them behind bars. And there was always the suspicion that Fegan, at least, was a tout, an informer, for one arm of the law or another. At one stage when we had run a front page headlined 'ULSTER'S SEVEN DEADLY SINNERS', we named the seven top drugs dealers in the Province. Speedy was top of the list. When Campbell and then Fegan were shot dead, drugs dealers and their cronies started blaming us.

But neither the *Sunday World*, nor any of its journalists, have ever believed in summary justice, kangaroo courts — call it what you will — and even less in summary execution. We have always believed the proper place for drugs dealers poisoning the young people of this country is in the courts, and then put behind bars.

However, the word got around in the drugs underworld that to talk to the *Sunday World*, or to be written about in the *Sunday World* in connection with drugs, was to guarantee 'a wooden overcoat'.

That's bullshit. The drugs scene still leaks like a sieve: sources still keep popping up constantly, tipping us off, giving us information, even from behind the prison walls on their mobile phones. 'No honour among thieves' does thieves a grave injustice when it comes to drugs dealers!

Anyway, in this bar, this punter struts right up and says into my face: 'McDowell, after what you had done to Brendan Campbell, I hope you die a slow death ...' I'm a pacifist. Sometimes. So I didn't react. Sometimes, when you can sense there's a 'team' of them, you're better not to. Knives and broken bottles can do a lot of damage.

But that was the line the druggies liked to propagate: that we in the *Sunday World* were responsible for what DAAD or other killer gangs did to them.

But we didn't do it to Campbell, Fegan or any of them.

They did it to themselves.

And, ironically, as the Provos who shot them would say, they, themselves alone, were responsible.

7

Brendan 'Speedy' Fegan

The second of the 'Terrible Twins', 'Speedy' Fegan had been a crook, a 'wide boy', since his teens growing up in the border tinderbox town of Newry. He cut his teeth on crime, flitting between Newry and the Southern town of Dundalk, just six miles across the border in the Republic of Ireland. Dundalk, as Fegan grew up, was known as 'El Paso', because of the number of top Provos who had fled the North and were living in hiding from the Northern and British security forces there. Bombers, snipers, top terrorist strategists — they all flitted back and forth between Newry and Dundalk.

Fegan rubbed shoulders with many of them. But then he also may have rubbed them up the wrong way. Instead of joining the IRA, he started dealing in drugs, and at the age of fifteen, because of his dabbling in that dangerous game and his other criminal activities, dubbed 'antisocial' by the IRA, he was ordered out of his home town of Newry, under death threat from what he called the 'Bon Jovies' — the Provies.

It was then he really started cutting his teeth on the cutting edge of Ulster's most deadly and dangerous crime: drugs. Fegan hooked up with Brendan 'Bap' Campbell. Campbell and Fegan became bosom buddies. They were photographed sharing a hired stretch limousine, which took them to the Dublin races while both supped expensive American beer, bedecked in gold necklaces, gold earrings, gold watches and gold bracelets. They even featured in a front-page picture, carried in the *Sunday World*, which was later to cost another man his life.

He was Frankie Turley, another ODC (Ordinary Decent Criminal) who happened to fall in with Fegan. Turley was a crook, an armed robber, whose first real crime of note was when he and his cohorts held up and robbed the credit union in his own community where he grew up. For that, he was ostracised by the folk in that community, the tight-knit Catholic enclave of Short Strand in East Belfast. But eventually Turley was to pay with his life — when 'Speedy' Fegan put a bounty on his head for providing the limousine picture to the *Sunday World*.

Frankie Turley had survived other life-threatening scenarios, not least when he and a team of accomplices tried to rob a bookmaker's shop on Belfast's Falls Road. They didn't know that an SAS undercover squad was waiting outside, believing Turley's team were a top, gun-toting IRA cash-and-carry squad. The rest of Turley's team were shot dead, one of them as he sat in the driving seat of the getaway car. Turley, always trigger-quick when it came to improvisation, lay down on the betting shop floor, pretending he was one of the customers who had been ordered to belly-flop on to their faces at gunpoint. (One of the weapons in the gang's possession was, it later turned out, a gun that had a special trace on it placed either by military intelligence or MI5.) When regular soldiers eventually arrived on the scene of what was then a bloodbath, they ordered the betting shop to be cleared. Turley walked out, his black balaclava, which he had used in the raid, stuffed down the front of his shirt. He had already got rid of his weapon — there were some claims that it was a 'dummy', or replica, gun — by sliding it across the floor and as far away from his as possible. A code of silence, like the Mafia *Omertà*, governed republican West Belfast at the time. This meant that although some of the punters knew what Turley was doing at the time, no one was going to 'turn tout' to 'the Brits' or the 'black bastards' of the RUC. Frankie Turley simply walked away on that occasion.

But when Speedy Fegan ordered him dead, he walked nowhere. In fact, he was kneeling at the side of a guns 'hide', extracting weapons for another planned armed robbery, when two assassins, contracted to kill for Fegan's £20,000 bounty, struck. Turley's assassins had another reason to want the gang boss dead. The £20,000 on offer from Fegan was simply, in their eyes, a 'bonus', because Turley had double-crossed them following an earlier Belfast burglary. His criminal cohorts later found out about that because Turley was living too high on the hog. They believed he stole cash from a stash secreted away from another robbery.

So when Frankie Turley bent over the guns hide near a railway embankment on the Larne–Belfast line near Newtownabbey, six miles from Belfast city centre, he thought he was merely going to do another job. He knelt down to get the guns out of the underground hide. He was on his knees. He didn't know that one of his killers had hidden a sawn-off shotgun up the sleeve of his coat. The cold-hearted killer slid it silently down. Frankie Turley mightn't even have heard the squeeze of the trigger or the blast of the gun as he was 'Judassed' from behind — shot, lethally, in the back.

Just one other man heard the blast. He was sitting, sweating, in a car not far away. There was a reason for that: he had driven the Turley trio to the secluded spot where the guns were hidden. But he was completely unaware that Frankie Turley was to be executed. On hearing the blast, he drove off at high speed. The two assassins were flummoxed, but not for long. They even had the cool heads to carry Frankie Turley's body over to the nearby railway line and roll it down the embankment. That's where it was later discovered, close to the busy railway line. The two killers escaped on foot. The date of their deadly 'bounty hunters' mission was 12 June 1988. They later 'did a runner' across the border.

Frankie Turley's widow, Donna, knew where they were in hiding. She had spirit, and she was unforgiving. At one stage, she offered to take us to the County Donegal seaside town where the killers were holed up, and point them out. However, while police got most of the full story of Frankie Turley's untimely demise, there was insufficient evidence to prosecute. Nothing could be proved about Speedy Fegan's 'bounty'.

Speedy was still out there. Still dealing. Still having a ball with his flash cars, flash women, and flashing rolls of ill-gotten cash. But, as the Provos' maxim says, *Tiocaidh Ar Lá* — Our Day Will Come — and so Fegan's final day of reckoning was to come.

The Provos had passed a death sentence on him for a 'crime' committed while he was drunk. He had fallen foul of them by losing more and more caches of drugs as other drugs barons turned on him. There was little wonder or surprise in that. The old adage 'no honour among thieves' applies more to drugs dealers, jealous of each other's operations or envious of a rival's 'turf', than to any other sector of the criminal underworld.

But the rumour was that Speedy had lost one huge drugs cache too many. That was £250,000 worth of LSD tablets, nabbed by the police on a road near the pink-painted Sheepbridge Inn, an eye-catching establishment on a bad bend on the North side of

Newry on the main Belfast–Dublin road. The word on the street was that an IRA veteran in South Armagh — a cattle-smuggling, diesel-oil-running, arms-dealing, top Provo terrorist — had 'diversified' into drugs. The word was that he had bankrolled the LSD shipment to come into Ulster. And, the drugs grapevine had it, he was not amused when the whole shebang was seized after a tip-off to the RUC Drugs Squad. 'He was f*****g livid,' one source told us, 'spitting blood and bile. Threatening to have Speedy kneecapped — or worse.'

Speedy was called to a reckoning. He owed the top terrorist and his organisation money — lots of it. So he was told: 'Keep doing your business. Find the money to get more drugs in somewhere. But when you bring them in, we want a cut.' Speedy was told to pay the Provos their 'cut' of whatever deals he was doing every two months.

Said one drugs source in Newry: 'Those payback sums were not insubstantial. They were around £10,000 every two months that Speedy had to come up with. That's sixty grand a year. Some whack of money to pay out. Some pressure,' the source said, before adding: 'But at that time, the Provos were getting into everything in Newry. There was very little moving down there — from smuggling cattle, pigs and sheep (later to bring foot-and-mouth disease and spark an agricultural industry red alert throughout Ulster and the Republic), to selling illegal diesel and oil, to legit 'front' businesses, to money-laundering scams involving millions of pounds — that the Provos weren't into, in one way or another.'

Speedy Fegan was struggling by this stage. After losing a string of drugs shipments, he was finding it very difficult to raise the initial capital that would allow him to buy large consignments in Amsterdam or Spain, or deal with the 'main men' in Dublin, and get back into the big league again. When he missed a payment to the Provos, he was called to account. He was ordered to go and see a senior republican member active in South County Down.

Speedy had a long memory. He had been ordered out of his native town as a teenager. And here he was again, a drugs entrepreneur, independent, in his own eyes a 'made man' — self-made, that is — living life to the full, living it as *he* wanted to, no strictures, no control, but a neat lifestyle. He even had a luxury apartment in the sleepy town of Moira, County Down, once voted Ulster's Best Kept Small Town, and a haven for stockbrokers and bankers. And now he was being made to kow-tow, to touch the forelock, to the Provos again.

Speedy's resentment burned a hole in his belly. He stoked his fiery gut of anger by getting drunk. Then he went and got a gun. That was easy in those days. A few quid, a gun, and a few bullets to put in it. He tucked the weapon down the back of the belt in his trousers. And he went to see the senior republican.

There is an old Ulster saying, beloved by 'the Big Man', the Rev. Ian Paisley, and his Free Presbyterian flock: 'When the drink's in, the wit's out.' So it proved with Speedy Fegan. When the going over the bi-monthly stipend got hot, Fegan pulled the gun from under another designer pullover. He put it to the republican's head. 'Any more hassle from you or your kind,' he told the go-between, 'and I'll blow your f*****g head off.' Fegan stuck the gun back in his belt and left, the smell of the Budweiser beer he had earlier guzzled still fresh on the republican's face. But with the drink in him, Speedy didn't realise that he had just signed his own death warrant.

The last time I saw Speedy Fegan alive was in Belfast one afternoon when I was on my way to the City Hall. Ironically, I was going there to interview the European Union's newly appointed 'Drugs Czar', Torgny Petersen, one of the Directors of the European Cities Against Drugs (ECAD) organisation. He was on a whistle-stop courtesy tour of Belfast, Dublin and Cork. (Incidentally, during my interview, Mr Petersen put Ireland close to the top of the league for drugs abuse in the EU — fourth behind Holland, Germany and the UK.)

Anyway, I was cutting through a city-centre side street on my way to the City Hall when Fegan, known to be a natty dresser, walked out of a men's clothes shop close to Callendar Street. Solidly built, he stopped, and stared at me as I went to walk past.

I stared back. 'Do I know you?', I asked … knowing damn well who it was, even though he had his hair bleached dirty blond at that stage.

'You should,' Speedy shot back, 'I'm never out of your f*****g paper!'

And as we stood face-to-face, he said: 'You're going to get me killed.'

'No,' I replied, 'you're going to get yourself killed. You're poisoning the youngsters of this country.'

At that, he pulled down the neck of a designer crew neck sweater he was wearing. There were two lumps on his chest, like big boils.

'You got me this,' he said.

'No, you got yourself that,' I said.

'F**k you,' he said. 'You're a hypocrite. You drink, don't you? Alcohol's a drug, too …'

'Yes, I do,' I said. 'But then, I'm forty-nine years of age (as I was then), and I can make the decision as to whether to have a few pints of Guinness as an adult. But I am not a fourteen-year-old standing outside a school gate being supplied E tabs by one of your hood friends.'

Speedy lost the rag at that. He started ranting and raving, hurling insults as he walked away down the street. As clutches of gaping downtown shoppers stopped to watch and listen, I shouted after him: 'You're a child killer, Fegan!' He stopped, as if to come back. I urged him: 'Come on back — and we'll deal with it here and now.' He turned on his heel and walked away, perhaps remembering the last time he'd been in a fist fight on the streets, when his own mates turned on him in Belfast's Golden Mile, gave him a hiding, and then took the keys of his new, precious 'boy racer' car from him … and drove it away.

That was the last time I saw Speedy Fegan, outside the back of BHS in downtown Belfast when, at least, he had the balls to take me on, face-to-face.

The two lumps in his chest were two bullets still there from the first assassination attempt by the IRA.

Just a few nights previously, he was billeted up in a flat at the top of Belfast's Bradbury Place, just on the tip of Belfast's drugs-haunted Golden Mile. A gunman went into the four-storey brick building. Fegan must have known him, because when he knocked at the door, Speedy partially opened it. The gunman started firing with a .22 pistol — not the most popular would-be assassin's weapon of all time. Speedy took up to four slugs. But he lived.

And, strangely, he didn't head for the nearest hospital, which was the Belfast City Tower Block just a quarter of a mile away on the Lisburn Road. Instead, a friend drove him, wounded and bleeding, to a police station. And it wasn't the nearest police station, either. Instead, Speedy was ferried right across town, to the Musgrave Street police station, which is the main city centre base for CID detectives.

Why there? Why that much longer journey when he was shot, in pain, and losing blood?

There was speculation afterwards in the drugs underworld that Speedy then had finally signed his own death warrant with the Provos. There was speculation, perhaps to prove lethal, that Fegan had turned police tout. And the Provos, above all else, don't like, and have never tolerated, touts. So it was that Speedy first went to the police, and then to hospital. He had a couple of bullets removed. But he signed himself out before two more could be cut out by a surgeon a couple of days later. The reason for signing himself out? Says a then accomplice: 'He knew he was going to be shot dead sometime. He knew he had a lucky escape once. But to stay in a ward in a hospital bed would make him too easy a target. He had to get out.'

He wasn't to survive the second shooting, when the main Provo 'hitman' used a proved, tried and trusted assassin's tool: a deadly 9mm handgun.

It was on a Sunday afternoon shortly afterwards. The Provos exacted their own, very special, and very permanent, kind of retribution.

Fegan was at his happiest around horses. He loved them. Especially trotting ponies. He loved to gamble, and go to the races — as proved by the picture of him and Brendan Campbell in the back of the stretch limo on their way to Leopardstown racecourse in Dublin. But trotting races were his first love. With his access to easy cash, Fegan had splashed out £15,000 to buy a trotting horse just that week. Word got around the border town of Newry. Although exiled from there as a teenager, he took pride in evading the Provos' ban on him and going back to his old haunts. And he flaunted his presence and wealth at times. Never more so than on that fateful Sunday.

Fegan had returned to Newry with his new pony, knowing that Travellers were setting up a series of races. They threw down a challenge to race his pony against one of their best. It was a gauntlet Fegan could not resist. A harness-trap trotting race was arranged on the dual-carriageway running between Newry and the nearby Carlingford Lough port of Warrenpoint. Speedy's pony performed well. But it was beaten. So was Speedy's bet on his own horse. He lost thousands. But he took it in good part. He headed for the pub, with the Travellers he'd been jousting against.

And after a few pints, Fegan thought of a ruse to get some of his losses back. His horse may have been beaten in the four-legged race. But now, he offered the owner of the winning pony a two-legged race — himself, Speedy, against the Traveller, in an Olympic-style one hundred metre sprint along the banks of the Newry Canal. The craic, and the banter, was 'mighty' as they say. Most of the punters in the pub piled out to watch the sprint spectacle. Speedy, who prided himself on his fitness, won the race, and lifted the wager. It wasn't as much as he'd lost earlier in the horse-trotting race. But there was merriment and mirth in the handing over of the money, and at least some pride had been restored. The crowd went back to the cosiness of the Hermitage Bar. Drinks were ordered. Pints were drunk. The banter and bevvies flew.

But the next thing to fly were bullets. Two IRA 'hitmen' calmly walked into the bar. Fegan spotted them instantly, and, even though they were heavily disguised, he screamed: 'It's the Provies!' They were to be his last, dying words. The gunmen fired a total of twenty-one shots. They hit Fegan a total of fifteen times. Nine of the 9mm bullets smashed through Fegan's face.

In fact, the baby-faced drugs baron's death had been planned well in advance. Weeks before, the Provos abducted one of Fegan's close associates. He was held and interrogated about his high-flying drugs baron friend. The man agreed under duress to pass on vital information about Speedy's movements, particularly his movements during trotting-horse meetings. Fegan's murder was planned to the very last detail. Nothing was left to chance.

The killing was organised by the IRA's Commanding Officer in Belfast, who, although overseeing the operation, did not actually take part in the killing himself. The top Provo, who is a veteran assassin with the IRA front organisation Direct Action Against Drugs (DAAD), was a member of the 'hit team' that four years earlier gunned down the first 'Godfather', Mickey Mooney, in a Belfast pub. The Belfast CO hand-picked the 'hit team' to take out Speedy Fegan. First, he chose a member of the IRA who had carried out the Mooney shooting along with him. This experienced gunman earned his initial 'stripes' on Halloween night, 31 October 1992, by blowing away Sammy Ward, a former activist in the rival Irish People's Liberation Organisation (IPLO). That bloodletting took place in the Sean Martin's GAA club in Beechfield Street in the Short Strand area of East Belfast. The attack on Ward was part of a major IRA purge against the IPLO during what became known as 'The Night of the Long Guns', because the Provos had used rifles for kneecappings on some of their sixty-odd victims. The IRA later branded many of them drugs dealers. Ward was the only victim to die as a result of the sweeping, dead-of-night operation. The intention was to wipe out the IPLO. It succeeded. Just five days later, on 4 November, the leader of the IPLO's Belfast brigade released a statement saying the terror gang was being disbanded. As a result of singling out and shooting Sammy Ward on that night, the

IRA assassin, although being 'blooded' in his first killing, knew what he was doing, and was subsequently used in other face-to-face assassinations.

And it was in a copycat operation that, shortly after 1 p.m. on that spring Sunday, an IRA 'scout' walked casually into the Hermitage Bar as Fegan sat drinking with his cronies and the Traveller 'horsey men'. The 'scout', the Provos' tip-off man, was wearing designer-label casual clothing, the kind of style that Speedy himself was used to. He blended easily into the company, and was unnoticed as he ordered a drink at the bar. But he never even touched the glass. He spotted Speedy. He walked out without swallowing a drop. That was the signal for the Provos to strike.

Seconds later, two IRA men strode into the Hermitage Bar, which was packed with up to sixty people, many of them Travellers who were at the earlier, illegal trotting-horse race with Fegan and his cohorts — soon to become his funeral cortège. Heavily disguised, wearing false beards and moustaches, the gunmen walked briskly towards Fegan. Spotting the danger, the drugs baron grabbed a bar stool and then yelled: 'It's the Provies! It's the Provies!' But a huge 9mm bullet hit him smack on the forehead. It was like a scene out of a Hollywood movie.

Speedy Fegan immediately collapsed to the floor, 'like a coat falling off a hanger' according to one eyewitness at the time. As pandemonium broke out all around, the first gunman — the same killer who had shot both Ward and Mickey Mooney — continued to fire at Fegan, hitting him no less than *nine* times in the face and putting *six* slugs in his chest. The second gunman fired a volley of shots in the air to ensure that no one dared distract the assassin. A total of twenty-one bullets were fired, their shells later picked up by RUC anti-terror squad detectives.

The two-man 'hit team' then left the bar, and threw their weapons into the back seat of a waiting Volkswagen Golf car, which sped off. It is not known if the killers jumped in as well. Another getaway car may have been waiting — splitting the guns from the gunmen, a classic Provo tactic. Within minutes, the assassins were safely across the border, and into the Republic, taking them out of the clutches of the immediate RUC follow-up dragnet. Although both were Belfastmen, they had been living in Dundalk — also known as 'El Paso' — for some time. The seasoned IRA man who shot Speedy had moved to Dundalk after going on the run when he was identified carrying out a so-called 'punishment attack' in the Markets area of Belfast, close to Short Strand. The second gunman, who fired into the ceiling of the Hermitage Bar, was from the Ardoyne area of Belfast, but he had also been living in Dundalk for a number of years after going on the run when he was wounded during an IRA attack on North Queen Street RUC station, within walking distance of Belfast City Hall. A blood-stained jacket belonging to him was found at the scene.

The IRA carried out the murder of Speedy Fegan on a strictly 'no claim, no blame' basis — a hallmark of previous DAAD operations. The reason was simple: so as not to affect Sinn Féin's drive towards political acceptability and, in their eyes, political respectability.

8

Frankie 'Studs' Lanigan

'Where's the shooter?'

The words may have sounded like they were written on the pages of a cheap American crime novel about bootleggers and gangsters in Chicago during prohibition. Instead, they were to signal the prohibition on a man living out the rest of his life. It was in the early hours of 31 May 1998 in Dungannon, County Tyrone, over 3,000 miles away from Chicago. The gunman who asked for 'the shooter' outside the Glengannon Hotel disco on the outskirts of Dungannon was Frankie 'Studs' Lanigan, the man who had set up Brendan 'Bap' Campbell three months before.

The place that the shooting story was told was Belfast Crown Court in February 2000, by witness Gregory Mark Fox, who had gone to the disco with Lanigan and two women.

But the story of how he handed the lethal 9mm pistol to Lanigan in the car park of the Glengannon Hotel was not to unfold until almost two years after the cold-blooded murder, which the police said at the time they believed was drugs related.

Lanigan, aged thirty-three when the Glengannon nightclub shooting occurred, was no stranger to the gun. Or being the victim of the gun. The terror gang, Irish National Liberation Army (INLA), tried to murder him in 1995. He had been known to be at least on the fringes of both the INLA and the equally ruthless killer gang the Irish People's Liberation Army.

These two gangs had waged savage republican internecine feuds against each other, leaving a litany of brutal killings across Belfast, and elsewhere. At one stage the wife of the former leader of the INLA, Mary McGlinchey, was gunned down in front of her children as she bathed them in her Dundalk home. Her husband, Dominic 'Mad Dog' McGlinchey, was in Portlaoise jail at the time. Both man and wife originally hailed from South Derry. When Mary was buried in Bellaghy, it was at the height of the internal feuding. Armed troops and police lined the walls of the cemetery, fearing one faction would open up on each other — even at Mary McGlinchey's graveside. But there were known terrorists, from each side in the feud, who turned up. There was no trouble that day, a day in the tiny village of Bellaghy when you could actually bite on the tension as the army helicopter, with its 'heli-telly' spy-in-the-sky camera taking pictures, hovered just feet above the churchyard, the clatter of its blades almost drowning out the by then ritual orations read out at the graveside. That grave was to be re-opened later, to take the remains of Mary McGlinchey's husband Dominic. He was released from Portlaoise jail, to live, and die, in Drogheda, County Louth. He was taken out, as they say, by a hitman, who has never been caught. Whether 'Mad Dog' McGlinchey was by then dabbling in the jealously guarded drugs racket himself, whether he had tried to muscle in on protection rackets, or whether his past had simply caught up with him is still a matter of conjecture. But one thing is certain: Frankie 'Studs' Lanigan knew both Mary and Dominic McGlinchey.

In his time, Lanigan had been linked to feuding INLA men and proven terrorist killers Gerard 'Dr Death' Steenson and Hugh 'Cueball' Torney. In fact, he had had a lucky escape in December 1995, when the INLA tried to assassinate him as he sat eating dinner in his mother's house in Cairn Street, off the Lower Falls Road.

The district, close to the infamous Divis Tower block of flats (a known haven for drugs dealers and gangs of Belfast 'hoods' — thieves, joyriders, car hijackers, and knife- and gun-wielding Bronx-style teenage gangs) had seen many murders down the years of what the IRA called 'The Long War'. Indeed, a gable wall close to Cairn Street on the front of the Falls Road bore, for almost thirty years, the huge painted slogan: 'THE LONG WAR — VICTORY TO THE IRA!'

That pre-Christmas night at his mother's home, two masked gunmen from the INLA burst through the front door. As Lanigan dropped his knife and fork on the spuds and sausage he was eating, they opened up with a handgun and a sawn-off shotgun. The sawn-off shotgun was a sign they intended to get up close, make sure 'the job' was done right.

But Lanigan wasn't only built like a whippet. He could move like one. He was sinewy, slippery and speedy. He ducked and dived, and bolted for the kitchen and back doors. He got hit, badly. His right arm was almost shattered; his left hand and wrist were peppered with pellets from the flying shotgun cartridges. But he got out the back door of his mother's house and stormed into a neighbour's home. And as the gunmen rampaged after him, he squeezed through a window in that house — even though he must have been in agony — and ran for his life.

INLA sources claimed, at the time, that Lanigan was a drugs baron. He denied it point-blank. He claimed he was targeted by the gun gang because he had been in a fight with one of its leaders.

And it was a fight at the Glengannon Hotel nightclub that was to claim doorman John Knocker's life — killed, at point-blank range, with the 9mm pistol that Lanigan, again bloodied, asked Gregory Martin Fox for in the car park of the hotel in the early hours of a summer morning on 31 May 1998. Door 'bouncer' John Knocker was then aged twenty-two. He was a known 'hardman' from the Provo heartland of the Whiterock district at the top of the Falls Road in Belfast. An ex-prisoner himself, he was known, in Belfast parlance, to 'take no prisoners' when it came to dealing with bully boys, drunks, thugs or drugs dealers.

Security sources say Frankie Lanigan went to the Dungannon disco that night to deal in drugs. But, as Belfast Crown Court was told, he also went with a gun in his entourage. Our sources claim Lanigan had been ejected from the nightclub the weekend before, because the bouncers 'knew his form', as they say. So he went back the following weekend. He went into the nightclub. There was an altercation. Then a fight. Lanigan got a hiding. He was battered. And he was bloodied.

At the Crown Court case on Friday, 24 February 2000, Gregory Martin Fox, then aged twenty-seven, was found not guilty of murdering John Knocker. But he pleaded guilty to a string of crimes related to the shooting. He admitted giving the gun to Lanigan, although he claimed he didn't know it was real. He confessed in court to assisting an offender by driving Lanigan from the scene of the crime. He held his hands up to the charge of helping to dispose of the weapon. And he pleaded guilty to possession of a 9mm pistol and ammunition under suspicious circumstances.

It was Fox, aged twenty-seven at the time of the court case, and whose address was given as Riverdale Park South,

Andersonstown (not too far from where murder victim John Knocker lived) who told of battered Lanigan 'staggering' across the car park to where he was standing with his girlfriend, Nuala Delaney, then aged eighteen. The court was told that Lanigan walked straight up to Fox and demanded: 'Where's the shooter?'

'When that evidence was given,' a court reporter later told us, 'the words bounced like dumb-dumb bullets off the walls ...'

Fox was later sentenced. His girlfriend, Delaney, from The Manor, Black's Road, also in West Belfast, pleaded guilty to assisting an offender by obtaining a change of clothing for Lanigan and having a firearm in suspicious circumstances. She too was later sentenced

There is no doubt who the police believe was responsible for the shooting of John Knocker. When he was shot by the INLA back in 1995, Lanigan fled for a while to England. He said that was to protect his family from reprisals. Now, he is believed to be a fugitive in the Irish Republic. John Knocker, a hard man, had some hard acquaintances. They are said to have long memories. Frankie 'Studs' Lanigan has become a fugitive again. But this time, it is to protect himself. Both from John Knocker's connections, and from Northern Ireland murder squad detectives still hunting him after it was said in court that he issued the self-incriminatory line just seconds before John Knocker was shot dead: 'Where's the shooter?'

Officially, at the time of writing, the Royal Ulster Constabulary were refusing to comment on their manhunt for Lanigan for fear of prejudicing any future legal proceedings. But, like Lanigan's cryptic request for the killer weapon, the charges admitted to in the Crown Court by Fox and Delaney speak for themselves. And the front page lead story in the *Irish News*, the Belfast morning paper, in February 2000, which carried the dramatic picture illustrating Lanigan's INLA assassination bid wounds, and reporting what was said in the Knocker murder court case, pulled no punches. The main headline, carried beside Lanigan's picture, blasted: 'ON THE RUN — GUNMAN NAMED AS CLUB KILLER'.

9

The Victim

'From what I have heard in this court today, you would think Belfast is being run by drugs dealers ...'

The words did not come from a frustrated policeman. Nor were they born from the futility of a probation officer trying to keep drugs criminals, many of them still teenagers, in check. Nor, indeed, did they come from a magistrate or judge trying to do something similar.

The cold, calculated words came from someone whose job is to evaluate and summarise the evidence in front of him succinctly and to the point. He is the Coroner for the Greater Belfast area, Mr John Leckey. And the evidence presented to him has to be as cold as the corpses of the dead once they're on the mortician's marble slab. So Mr Leckey is not one for mincing his words. And he doesn't believe in pretty prose, either.

So it was that Coroner Leckey was conducting the inquest into the death of ready-mix concrete lorry-driver Gerard McKay. And it was after hearing evidence about the death of the twenty-three-year-old that Mr Leckey made the quote carried above: a quote that was to hit the headlines after the coroner's court case.

But first, the tale of a fighter. He's also called Gerry McKay. And he's a silver-haired car dealer who is the young lad's father. He believes that his son was murdered. He believes that the late Paul Daly, a drugs dealer known in Belfast as 'King Coke', murdered his son.

Mr McKay believes that on the night before his son died, Gerard Junior left his flat at 400 Ormeau Road. That part of the Ormeau Road is quiet and respectable. It is not to be confused with the annual Orange marching impasse at the Lagan Bridge further on down the road, where the Orangemen from Ballynafeigh try to march through the mainly nationalist Lower Ormeau Road. Gerry McKay, his wife and the rest of his family live just a few hundred metres from the flat, part of a big, red-bricked, detached suburban townhouse turned into a number of apartments and bed-sits. They were, and still are, a close-knit family. Gerry McKay believes that his son was neither a drugs user nor a dealer. But he also believes that 'King Coke' was in the flat that fateful night. He was there for a reason.

'I believe that he wanted to bully my son into becoming a drugs courier for him,' said Mr McKay. 'Gerard was driving a ready-mix concrete truck. Dealers were already using at least one Royal Mail van for moving drugs. Great cover. The police or the Customs & Excise people would never think of stopping a Royal Mail van. The police's job is to protect such vans and their contents, after all.'

A ready-mix concrete truck would also provide 'great cover' for moving drugs around. Protect the drugs by wrapping them in bubble-wrap, tape them, throw them in the concrete-mixing drum in the back of the big lorry, and what policeman is ever going to ask the driver to pour a tonne of wet concrete all over a main road or traffic artery? And, if the drugs were taken to a certain location, they could be fished out when needed.

The only thing was, Gerry McKay Junior said no. That irked 'King Coke', big time.

Gerry McKay hasn't rested since his son's death. He has painstakingly built up a network of contacts, some of them on the seedy side of society. And he has relentlessly pursued the goal of justice for what he sees as his son's murder. From his contacts, here is the picture he paints of his only son's last few hours.

'King Coke' was 'narked' at Gerard Junior's refusal to become a courier. He refused point-blank and went out for a Chinese takeaway meal. He also bought a bottle of mineral water. When he returned to the flat, 'King Coke' was back. Gerard went to the kitchen to unpack his Chinese meal. He left the mineral water in the living room of the flat. His father believes that that was when Daly 'Judassed', or spiked, the bottle of mineral water.

He has good evidence to back up that theory. The pathologist at his son's inquest gave evidence to Coroner Leckey that when a post-mortem was carried out on Gerard Junior's body, there was the equivalent of ten E tabs in his system. The pathologist said that would be a fatal dose. The pathologist also told the inquest that there were some dregs left in the mineral water bottle found in the flat the morning after Gerard Junior died. There was the equivalent of another — an *eleventh* — Ecstasy tablet found dissolved in that.

Gerry McKay says: 'I believe my son at first unknowingly started drinking the mineral water with the dissolved E tablets in it. Categorically, he was not involved in drugs himself. But I believe by refusing to become a courier for drugs pushers, he effectively signed his own death warrant. As the E tablets in the mineral water took effect, I believe my son became dazed and disorientated. And then I believe he was fed more of that mickey-finned [contaminated] water. I believe that that is how and why my son died.

I believe he was murdered.'

The coroner's court hearing the inquest into Gerard McKay's death was told that he died from a drugs overdose at around 4 a.m. Having listened to evidence presented to his court, the Belfast City Coroner John Leckey made his bombshell comment from the bench that 'it seems Belfast is being run by drugs dealers'. The DPP had previously been sent a police file on the death, but his department had decided that there was insufficient evidence to prosecute. Having listened to the evidence in his coroner's court, and later spoken personally to Mr McKay, Mr Leckey decided to send the witness depositions to the DPP's office with a view to the whole case being looked at again. The DPP called in an independent senior barrister to re-assess the case in view of the most unusual step taken by the coroner. Again, however, there was deemed to be insufficient evidence to mount a successful prosecution.

But Gerry McKay hasn't given up. He is still relentlessly pursuing the case. He has been to the Stormont Assembly, to tell his sad and sorry tale to assembly members like David Ervine of the Progressive Unionist Party and Monica McWilliams of the Women's Coalition. Both have listened, and pledged support in his campaign. Ms McWilliams has youngsters of her own, and, like legions of other Ulster parents, is fearful, to say the least, about bringing children up in an Ulster society now plagued by drugs and ruthless drugs dealers. David Ervine knows all about the violent aspect of drugs dealing. His own son was working, innocently, in a downtown Belfast club one night, 'trying to earn a few bob', when a gun gang murdered a doorman in cold blood.

Gerry McKay has also been to the Belfast bureau of the Human Rights Commission. They told him they will examine his case, and decide if they can take any action. He's been to the office of the new police Ombudsman, Nuala O'Loan, also in Belfast. He has been back to see Coroner John Leckey at his Newtownabbey headquarters. While there, he mentioned to Mr Leckey that he'd been to the police Ombudsman. Mr Leckey, still interested in the case, phoned Ms O'Loan's office, to be told that the McKay file was on her desk. By the time this book is published, things in the Gerry/Gerard Junior case may have moved on, in the official sense. And, as the sequel to this chapter shows, it has moved on unofficially, with the IRA murder of Paul 'King Coke' Daly.

I have talked often, and at length, with Gerry McKay. I went with him to Stormont to meet David Ervine and Monica McWilliams. I have also met Paul Daly. We met, face-to-face, in Jury's Inn in downtown Belfast. He denied, point-blank, that he had murdered Gerard McKay. I asked him if he would meet Mr McKay face-to-face, with me there as a witness, with a tape recorder in the middle, and allow Gerry McKay to ask him the same question — and more questions. At the time he said he would. And he claimed at that meeting that he was no longer dealing in drugs.

However, Hugh Jordan was with me. Hugh had run a story a couple of weeks previously in the *Sunday World* telling of how the Provos had tried to kill Daly in a central Belfast hotel. Two gunmen had walked into the hotel bar on a Sunday afternoon. They were dressed in business suits, shirts and ties. They were carrying briefcases. In the briefcases were guns. Fortunately for Daly, he had left the hotel bar — just seconds before the pair of gunmen walked in.

When we met him in Jury's, he confirmed a second murder bid incident to us. He said he was just feet away from driving

Baubles, bangles, beer — and bullets. Two of Ulster's first 'Godfathers' in the back of a stretch limousine, on their way to the races in Dublin. But both Brendan 'Speedy' Fegan and Brendan 'Bap' Campbell were among the first to die, cut down in a hail of bullets from Direct Action Against Drugs (DAAD) gunmen.

*The first drugs 'Godfather',
Mickey 'Money Bags'
Mooney, and the first to die
at the hands of a DAAD
killer gang.*

*Mickey Mooney's brother,
Liam 'Fat Boy' Mooney,
who was to take over the
mantle of 'Godfather' from
his murdered brother.*

Maxi McAlorum, 'Fat Boy's' side-kick. He was to witness his nine-year-old daughter's murder, on his knee.

Little Barbara McAlorum, shot dead at her home in Belfast. But her father was the gunmen's target.

LVF boss Billy 'King Rat' Wright: in a 'hard man' pose under an Orange arch in the Maze jail — where he was later murdered.

Billy Wright in civvies — shirt and tie — at a rally. Behind him is Portadown, Co. Armagh, lad Andrew Robb, later murdered during a bitter loyalist feud.

The assassin who took out Billy Wright behind bars: convicted killer Christopher 'Crip' McWilliams. Like Wright, he is a fitness fanatic, and is a former top member of the outlawed INLA.

Father of one of the drugs 'Godfathers'' victims, Gerry McKay Senior (centre), taking his campaign to Stormont with (left) David Ervine of the PUP, and Monica McWilliams of the Women's Coalition.

Gerard McKay Junior: his father, Gerry, believes his son was murdered by drugs 'Godfather' Paul Daly, later himself gunned down.

From porn queen to drugs 'Godmother': Nuèla Fitchie (left) with her mate 'June the Balloon' McKibbin, sunbathing topless in Spain.

Nuèla — who called herself 'Luella' for her live sex shows — in happier times, before she died after swallowing a drugs overdose in an English police cell.

Some of the Sunday World Belfast office staff, with then Secretary of State for Ulster, Mo Mowlam. She came to the office to show solidarity, after drugs 'Godfather' Brendan 'Speedy' Fegan ordered it to be firebombed.

Author Jim McDowell surveys the damage to the Sunday World Belfast office foyer after the attempted torching.

through a gateway into the back courtyard of a downtown Belfast club. But he said that at almost the last second, he got a warning (presumably by mobile phone) to speed away. He claimed a Provo hit team had been waiting in the courtyard, and that as soon as he and his cohorts in the car drove in, the IRA gang was going to slam the gate shut and then riddle their Mercedes car with gunfire. Later, Hugh and I checked out the story with our sources. It stood up.

Just afterwards, we believed a third attempt was to be made on this 'Godfather's' life. We got a tip-off that the IRA planned another 'Night of the Long Guns' on Halloween night, 31 October 2000. They were going to target, beat and expel another team of drugs dealers. But this time, instead of trying to shoot Daly, whom they'd already tried to 'touch for' twice, they were going to put a 'magnet' under his new jeep. That meant only one thing. A boobytrap, undercar bomb.

Halloween was to fall on the Tuesday night. We splashed with the story on the previous Sunday: 'HALLOWEEN HORROR PLANNED' was the front-page headline. Daly got the message. So did the Provos. Their killer plan, their Halloween 'Night of the Long Guns' had been thwarted. It didn't happen. As I said before, we don't believe in summary justice, or summary execution.

And as for the thanks we got from Daly, well, the next time he saw one of us he was involved in another story, and he said: 'Why don't you tell the truth for a change in that paper?' My answer was short, and simple: 'You wouldn't know the truth if it hit you smack up the face ...'

And as for his compassion — two years to the day after Gerry McKay buried his son, Daly walked up to Mr McKay in the street and asked him a question as cold-hearted and mocking as any bastard could pose: 'Is your son still dealing in drugs where he is now?' No wonder Gerry McKay is frustrated, committed, campaigning, and still furious ...

It is good to report that at the time of writing, Gerry had, at last, made a significant breakthrough.

The new Police Ombudsman for Northern Ireland — lawyer Nuala O'Loan — had put two of her investigating officers on Mr McKay's case. And when the *Sunday World* published that fact on 11 March 2001, it certainly caused a ripple of something more than consternation on the drugs dealers' front.

Unfortunately, it also led to more unsavoury threats being made to contacts who had been supplying both Gerry and myself with information. At the time of writing — the day before writing this, in fact — I was forced to make a formal approach to the RUC to report a series of threats in case anything happened to Gerry, or me, or one of our contacts who, on the previous day, had to have a police escort to take his kids to school after he was informed of a death threat.

The Sequel: Part 1

'Get out of the car! For f**k's sake get out of the car!'

Those were the last, despairing, dying words uttered by the Belfast drugs Godfather, Paul Daly, on the bright, sunlit spring afternoon of 4 May 2001.

At precisely five minutes past four, a friend and colleague of mine, Darwin Templeton, then Chief Reporter of the *Belfast Telegraph*, phoned me on my mobile. 'I've some news for you,' Darwin said. 'Paul Daly has just been shot dead.'

I had been expecting it. The word on the street was that the IRA were still looking for Daly, after their earlier abortive attempts to assassinate him. But I was still shocked.

'When?' I asked.

'3.59 p.m.' said Darwin.

'Where?' I asked.

'Almost outside the back door of the *Telegraph*, where I'm sitting now,' Darwin replied.

There was no point in going to the murder scene. It was only 400 metres, and across a couple of streets, away from where I was standing having a pint — ironically, with two off-duty detectives. But the first thing I did was to phone Gerry McKay.

I wanted to be the first to tell him, though not for any reasons of triumphalism. After all, it was another brutal tragedy. My stance, reiterated throughout this book, was that the place for drugs dealers like Daly was behind bars, not in a burial place, and certainly not put there by kangaroo courts sanctioning summary justice, and summary execution.

I eventually got Gerry. As I expected, he denounced the killing (of anyone), and took no great delight in the news that Daly, the man he believed murdered his son, had himself been murdered in cold blood. His attitude is reflected later in this Sequel.

As to the other reason for not rushing to the murder scene: well, it had happened in broad daylight on a Friday afternoon, carried out by two killers — bare-faced, and blatantly, not masked — wearing beige baseball caps and denim jackets. And I knew it would be splashed all over the Saturday papers.

It was, with page 1 headlines like 'KING COKE GUNNED DOWN' and 'EXECUTION' blaring off the front pages. There was also a picture of Daly, a blanket draped over his body, and his feet, in Timberland boots, lying at a grotesque angle. Those stories, and what transpired throughout the next day, the Saturday, tell the tale of the horror murder.

Daly's partner, Jacqueline Conroy, had been sitting in the car, a courtesy vehicle while Daly's own Range Rover jeep was in the garage being fixed, when two gunmen approached the car. One of them came right at the windscreen. She was in the passenger seat. Daly saw what was coming and he pushed her out of the passenger door. She escaped unscathed — except emotionally, of course. He tried to dive out the passenger side door after her. It was too late. His last words were: 'Get out of the car! For f**k's sake get out of the car!'

The Sequel: Part 2
'SHOT DRUG DEALER KILLED MY SON'

That was the four-deck headline printed on the front page of the Northern edition of the *Sunday World* on Sunday 6 May, less than two days after Daly was gunned down. We were the only paper to have a picture of Daly, taken outside court where he was facing a grievous bodily harm charge. He had beaten a man to a pulp and had put him in intensive care. So, his picture was on the front page.

Also for the first time was a photograph of the lad Gerry McKay believed Daly had murdered — Gerry's son, Gerard Junior.

As for the angle we took on the Daly killing: well, after all Gerry McKay and his family had been through, there was only one line for us to take: his. Thus, under that banner headline 'SHOT DRUG DEALER KILLED MY SON', the front-page write-off, leading into two pages inside, read:

Drugs Godfather Paul 'King Coke' Daly, gunned down in Belfast in broad daylight on Friday, was a murderer himself.

The thirty-eight-year-old ex-weightlifting champ who once converted part of his home into a gym, murdered Belfast lad Gerard McKay, then twenty-three, on the night of 28 November 1998.

Bully boy Daly laced a bottle of Evian water with *eleven* deadly 'E' tabs and forced the young lorry driver to drink almost every drop.

Gerard McKay's body was found at 4 a.m. the next morning. Daly later boasted about the killing while on drunken binges.

Since, Gerard's father, Gerry Snr, has campaigned relentlessly to get the man he is convinced murdered his son brought to justice.

That man was Daly, who in recent years became the No. 1 Public Enemy of the Ulster drugs underworld.

The *Sunday World* has backed Gerry McKay in his courageous campaign.

We have accompanied him to see Stormont politicians David Ervine and Monica McWilliams.

And we have been interviewed — just days before Daly's murder — by investigators from the new police Ombudsman's office in Belfast.

Those investigators are also probing claims:

- That he was a former Special Branch informer.
- That he was, until his death, setting up other top drugs dealers for Drugs Squad raids.
- That he walked away from a series of serious assault charges — including putting a man in intensive care after beating him over the head with a hammer, and then leaving him for dead in his own house.

There were four more stories on a double-page spread on pages 2 and 3 inside. The headline on the main story there was 'SHOT DEALER WAS KILLER WHO SPIKED 'E' DEATH MAN'S WATER', with a sub-heading reading 'But dead man's father says corrupt cops were involved in a cover-up'. That story read:

'Drugs Godfather Paul Daly, who was gunned down on Friday, forced a young Belfast man to drink a deadly concoction that cost him his life.

Gerard McKay (twenty-three) died in the early hours of 29 November 1998.

An inquest into his death was told that he had the equivalent of ten Ecstasy tablets in his system when he died.

After hearing evidence at the inquest, the Coroner, Mr John Leckey, declared that 'you would think that Belfast is being run by drugs dealers'.

The Coroner's Court also heard police evidence that three suspected drugs dealers were in Gerard McKay's flat at 400 Ormeau Road, Belfast, the night he died.

None of them, although notified, turned up at the inquest. One of them was Paul Daly.

Gerard McKay's father, Gerry Snr, believes Daly murdered his son by poisoning a bottle of Evian water he was drinking with at least eleven E tabs, and then forcing lorry driver Gerard to gulp most of it down while he held him by the throat.

He says he believes Daly wanted his son to act as a drugs courier — by transporting cannabis and pills wrapped in bubblewrap in the revolving barrel of his cement lorry — and that he wanted information from Gerard about a friend of his who had allegedly ripped off Daly for £20,000 in a drugs scam.

To this day, Gerry McKay is adamant his son was NOT a drugs dealer.

He is equally adamant that his son WAS murdered by Friday's murder victim, Paul Daly.

Mr McKay, fifty, has run a sustained and marathon campaign since his son's death to get justice.

The *Sunday World* has backed that campaign, setting up meetings for Gerry with Stormont MLAs David Ervine and Monica McWilliams.

The politicians followed that up with a visit to see a very senior officer at the RUC's Knock headquarters.

Plus, both the Human Rights Commission and the new police Ombudsman's office opened files on the McKay case.

Only last Wednesday, investigators from the Ombudsman's office had an hour-long meeting with a *Sunday World* reporter about the whole saga.

It is steeped in murky waters.

There are allegations that:

- Daly was a former Special Branch informer during the years of the terror war, and regarded himself as an 'untouchable' in terms of the law, threatening to 'lift the lid' on his time as a tout if he couldn't beat the rap on any charge.

- He consistently set up other top drugs dealers for Drugs Squad raids and seizures and grassed on a huge £1 million heroin deal.

- And that he walked away from a series of serious assault charges — including putting another bodybuilder and 'hard man' in intensive care after beating him over the head with a hammer, and leaving him for dead in his Laurelgrove Dale luxury bung-alow where he was still living until the time of his own death.

Other assaults included an attack on a young man delivering a Chinese carryout to one of his previous homes.

He accused the young lad of 'doing him' in 50p, chased him down the street, caught him, and beat him with a brick.

Mysteriously, charges against Daly for that were dropped.

And there was another assault, on a security man at a store in Bangor, County Down, where, mysteriously again, Daly was never brought to court.

But it was while Daly was being processed through the courts on the grievous bodily harm charge that our exclusive picture of him sitting at the driving wheel of his Mercedes was snapped.

On that day, he told me that there was no point in me being at the preliminary hearing in a Magistrate's court, because the grievous bodily harm charge would be dropped.

It wasn't. Even though 'approaches' were made to the victim to drop his complaint.

Daly went on to be prosecuted at Downpatrick Crown Court.

He eventually pleaded guilty. But he walked away from that, too, with a suspended sentence which left his victim — who later labelled Daly 'a cowardly bastard' – and Gerry McKay, angry.

But before then, as Gerry McKay stood on the steps of the Downpatrick courthouse, Daly brushed past him.

And he jibed at Gerry McKay: 'Is your son still dealing where he is now?'

Gerry McKay has consistently insisted that his son was not a drugs dealer, and was not involved in drugs in any way.

However, the insult was hurled on a very poignant date for the McKay family.

It was two years to the day that a still heartbroken Mr McKay buried his son in his grave.

Last night, Gerry McKay said: 'I never wanted anyone killed. I didn't want Paul Daly murdered.

'I just wanted justice.

'I do believe Paul Daly murdered my son.

'I still want the investigation to continue into everything that happened in that flat that night.

'I want records of who phoned my son, and when.

'I have already been told that the Sim card from my son's mobile has been lost.

'I can't understand that. It was ten days after my son's death before I was allowed into the flat.'

And the police Ombudsman's office is also looking into the murder of another man murdered by a drugs dealer.

The drugs baron was a cohort of Paul Daly's.

He stabbed another Belfastman, Hugh McKee, to death outside a taxi firm on the city's Antrim Road.

Before his death, Daly held weekly booze sessions, most Friday afternoons, in either a pub close to the centre of Belfast, a hotel in South Antrim, or another hotel in North Down.

Recently, we were told by security force sources that those meetings were 'under heavy surveillance'.

Daly missed one of those meetings last Friday ... and paid with his life.

But even at that, the maxim that there is no honour among thieves — or drugs dealers — held fast.

Yesterday morning, less than 18 hours after Paul Daly's

murder, two of his former cronies made an approach to *Sunday World*.

They were offering 'exclusive' pictures of him, and other sensitive information.

Their asking price? Twenty thousand pounds.

We refused the offer ...'

There were three other stories which appeared on that double-spread across pages 2 and 3.

Earlier in this chapter, before the sequel about Daly's death had to be added, I told how the Provos had tried to murder Daly before. So the second story was headlined: 'HOW SUNDAY WORLD SAVED DALY'S LIFE BEFORE'. It read:

The *Sunday World* saved drugs baron Paul Daly's life.

That was last Halloween.

The Provos had already tried to murder him twice before.

Daly confirmed those attempts himself.

He met — along with his 'minder' — crime correspondent Hugh Jordan and myself in the bar of Jury's Inn in the centre of Belfast.

The 'minder' paced about the bar wary of another assassination attempt as Daly, sweat streaming down his face, asked us if we were 'wired' — in other words, had we hidden microphones on us, or electronic devices from which our whereabouts could be traced.

We told both him and his prancing 'minder' not to be stupid.

But we were able also to tell Daly details of two of the three previous murder bids on him.

One, which we had reported shortly afterwards, was in a Belfast hotel.

It occurred on a Sunday, when two would-be assassins in business suits walked into the bar.

They carried briefcases. Inside, were handguns.

Their target was Daly. By good fortune — or on a mobile phone tip-off — he had left just minutes previously.

He confirmed that first murder bid to us.

Secondly, we told him that he had narrowly escaped death again when he was about to drive the car he then owned — a white Mercedes — into a parking space at the back of a nightclub.

This time, his mobile phone, never far from his ear at any time, took a call which warned him of the death trap — just seconds before his car was due to be sprayed with bullets.

He confirmed that, too.

But after that, we discovered a plot, leaked to us from republican sources, that the Provos planned another 'Night of the Long Guns' last Halloween night.

That was to be a repeat of an infamous night long before when, in a co-ordinated overnight campaign, Provo punishment squads swooped on the night of 31 October 1992 and blew away Sammy Ward of the IPLO.

Five bullets were pumped into his head . . . a carbon copy execution of the Provo 'hit' carried out on Paul Daly in Belfast's Stephen Street on Friday afternoon.

But *Sunday World* scuppered a similar 'Night of the Long Guns' plot last Halloween.

We were told then that the Provos planned another beating and punishment shooting purge of drugs dealers.

And that they planned to plant a bomb under Daly's new jeep — he had switched from the white Mercedes by then, because, underworld sources told us, he was 'fed up' reading about the Merc in the *Sunday World*.

The source's tip-off to us was that a 'magnet' was to be placed under the jeep.

In other words, he was to be killed with a boobytrap bomb under the plum-coloured Range Rover.

As we have stated before, this newspaper believes drugs dealers should be behind bars — not buried in graves after summary justice and summary execution meted out by paramilitaries or anyone else.

So two days before Halloween, on Sunday 29 October last, we ran a 'Provos Plan Halloween Horror' story on the front page.

We didn't name Daly as the car bomb target. But he got the message — again.

And when the Provos knew they'd been rumbled with the purge story leak, they called off their operation — meaning we saved Daly's life.

However, he knew he was a marked man.

The Provos decided against murdering him at his own home at Knockbracken in the Four Winds area of Belfast.

He lived in a fenced-off complex, with ornate gates at the entrance.

Our sources say the nature of the place made it too difficult to make a clean getaway.

And, as another story illustrates, Daly's plush bungalow was festooned with security cameras, alarms, and bullet-proof windows and doors.

Instead, the Provos prepared for a 'clean' hit, and a clean getaway.

They knew Daly called at a relative's house at Stephen Street in the heart of Belfast most Fridays to collect his wife.

She came from nearby Carrick Hill. He came originally from the Ardoyne in North Belfast.

Unfortunately, when the Provos struck — abandoning their stolen 'hit' car with false numberplates later in the heart of UFF chief Johnny Adair's Lower Shankill HQ — Daly's wife and young daughter were witnesses to his brutal murder.

That abandoning of the car in the Lower Shankill may have been meant to throw police off the scent of the real killers.

But yesterday a reliable source inside the republican movement told us:

'Make no mistake about it — it was us.'

Three weeks ago the Provos also murdered Derry drugs Godfather Christopher 'Cricky' O'Kane.

Then they shot original Godfather Mickey Mooney's son, Michael Jnr, four times.

And, a fortnight ago, they 'sixpacked' Belfastman Jim Lismore, shooting him through the elbows, hands and feet.

Mr Lismore told us then that he had been a drugs dealer, but had given it up over a year before his shooting.

And when Paul Daly met us in the Jury's Inn he told us the same: that he had given up drugs dealing after starting that criminal, and lucrative, pursuit while running teams of pub and club bouncers in Belfast.

But even, as they say, the dogs in the street knew that he had taken over from former murdered drugs 'Godfathers' like Mickey Mooney, Speedy Fegan, Brendan Campbell,

Paddy Farrell, and 'Big Edd' McCoy as the No. 1 'Godfather' in Ulster — and as Public Enemy No. 1 from the criminal underworld, as well.

Said one security source last night: 'The dogs in the street also knew that Paul Daly was still up to his neck in drugs dealing — and that his street nickname was 'King Coke'.

The third story on the spread was written by our News Editor, Richard Sullivan.

Less than twenty-four hours after Daly was gunned down in Stephen Street, at noon the next day, Saturday 5 May, the police staged a scene-of-crime Press conference. The top detective investigating the murder was there.

I was writing the rest of the stuff for the front and double-page spread, so Richard volunteered to go and cover the hard news-breaking angle at the police Press briefing. His story, summing up the savagery of what had happened less than twenty-four hours earlier, at this very spot in the heart of Belfast and less than half a mile from the City Hall, was headlined: 'DRUG LORD'S DAUGHTER HEARD HER DAD DIE.'

This is what he wrote:

Paul Daly's daughter may have passed her father's killers in the street. It has emerged that eleven-year-old Lindsay heard the shots and was running across the road at Carrick Hill — 50 yards from the murder scene.

Detectives believe she may have passed her father's killers as they fled.

Seconds later she saw her father's bullet riddled body lying on the footpath at Stephen Street.

She had been at a friend's house in the neighbourhood waiting to be collected by her parents.

She is believed to have heard up to eight shots.

RUC Detective Superintendent Philip Wright said Lindsay and Paul Daly's wife Jacqueline were in deep shock and extremely distressed.

'We were fortunate that there was not a second murder here,' he said.

'Paul's wife was in the car when the gunmen opened fire and was lucky to escape with her life.'

One of the gunmen walked in front of the victim's car and opened fire through the front windscreen. Daly's wife managed to scramble to safety through the passenger door of the blue Peugeot 206.

Daly desperately tried to get clear but his killers riddled him with bullets hitting him in the head and body.

The hardman's body was left slumped on the pavement.

DS Wright said detectives believe that the killers parked their car across the road at Carrick Hill and made their way to the murder scene on foot.

One of them opened fire with a handgun from the front of the car before making off towards Carrick Hill.

'The two suspects had difficulty getting across what is a very busy road.

'We want to talk to people who may have seen these men, who were not masked, as they tried to cross the road,' he said.

The killers used a silver Nissan car which was driven by a third man. The car was later found abandoned at Hopewell Avenue off the Crumlin Road.

It is understood the gang used an incendiary device to try and burn the vehicle out. But it failed to ignite and detectives are hoping forensic evidence will help lead them to the gang.

The police have refused to speculate on who was responsible for the attack but it is widely believed that an IRA hit squad was behind it.

'This is a busy area. There are business premises, bars, a snooker club and a very busy road. So even if people don't think they saw anything significant we would like to hear from them if they were in the district between 3 p.m. and 4 p.m. on Friday,' said DS Wright.

And there was one other story, with a picture, on that page. We had touched lucky. We knew Daly's house had been up for sale. It had an estate agent's sign outside, with the selling agency's name on it. We went into their website on the Internet. They had Daly's house on the website, pictures and all. With that picture, the story filed read:

'This is the luxury home of drugs dealer Paul Daly.

He had been living in the exclusive Laurelgrove development at Knockbracken in South Belfast.

It looks like an ordinary bungalow from the outside — except for the security cameras jutting out from the eaves of the house.

But it is situated in a specially fenced-off development which has ornate gates at the entrance, and which is described by estate agents as 'convenient' and 'quiet'.

It wasn't so quiet yesterday when reporters and photographers were told to 'f*** off' by the murdered drugs dealer's cronies.

Recently, Daly was trying to sell the house, at 'offers over £137,500'.

And though the exterior, with bullet-proof windows, is unprepossessing — even with the Range Rover in the driveway — the inside of the house, with its 'extensive use of natural timber, wooden floors', and its master bedroom with en suite shower room and 'luxury kitchen', is eye-opening . . . as our pictures of the interior show.

As the blurb from the estate agents selling the property said: 'We have no hesitation in recommending internal inspection to fully appreciate the numerous qualities of this fine property.'

And where was Mr Daly planning to move when he sold this house?

He told prospective buyers that he was moving to the even more exclusive stockbroker belt of Cultra in County Down.

Others thought he may have been trying to get out of Ulster altogether . . . and that he may have already bought a pub in Spain in partnership with another drugs dealer in England.

And all of this for a man who had no known means of visible income — although a court was told recently that he was the manager of a demolition company.

Although on Friday, the IRA made sure that it was his past, rather than his future, that caught up with him.'

The publication of that story, over three pages, and quite clearly designating Daly as a drugs 'Godfather', was to lead to an unexpected — and rather amazing – sequel.

The Sequel: Part 3
'Did you pay any of those scumbags £20,000 for pictures of Daly?'

It was Saturday morning, 12 May. I'd been into work early, had gone out for a jog to get my head showered — both figuratively and literally — in the rain, and was back in the office. My mate, and one of our photographers, a good lad called Conor McCaughley, had come into the office. He told me a woman had been on the phone for me. He said she wanted to talk to me about the stories we had run the previous Sunday about Daly. She had left a phone number.

I phoned it. To my astonishment, it was Daly's partner, Jacqueline Conroy, the mother of his children, including an infant who had died tragically only months old; he had swallowed a screw nail and choked to death before he could get to hospital.

I expected bile, hatred, animosity to spill down the phone line. Instead, Ms Conroy was cool, calm and collected. She said she wanted to see me, personally, at the family home at Knockbracken. I asked why. She replied with a question: 'Did you pay any of those scumbags £20,000 for pictures of Daly?'

Not Paul. Not 'my Paul'. Just 'Daly'.

I said I hadn't. She said if that was the case, and I was telling the truth, to come to her house and she would give me pictures of 'Daly' — she referred to him like that, using his surname throughout the subsequent hour-long interview at her home. I told her I'd be up at her house in half an hour.

I had my doubts about going. I feared that it could have been a set-up, to have me shot dead. I talked about it with the boys in the office. Big Richard Sullivan, the News Editor, was particularly compassionate, as is his wont.

'If you get the interview with her, and the pictures,' the big lad said, 'it will be a smashing splash (lead story) for the morning. But if you get shot dead … an even better story!'

So much for your mates and colleagues in times of trouble

and turmoil! Anyway, I said I was going, Conor said he was coming with me, and we went.

I knocked on the door of the Daly household.

Jacqueline Conroy was sitting behind venetian blinds, still drawn closed to signify the house was in mourning. She called out, 'Come on in, Jim.'

One thing the police had always warned us when we were under threat, or in danger before, was 'never walk in anywhere blind'. I didn't know what — or who — might be behind that door. But at least Conor was in the car at the kerbside. He had a mobile. He could summon help, fast, if anything happened.

It didn't. I walked in. Jacqueline Conroy was sitting alone on a settee in her living room.

This is the story that appeared the next day, Sunday 13 May, with her insisting throughout that her partner, 'Daly', was not a drugs dealer. The four-deck headline on the front page ran: 'LOVER TO NAME DALY'S KILLER'. The page 1 write-off, tagging into another double-page spread on pages 2 and 3, read:

The grieving partner of Provo murder victim Paul Daly last night told the *Sunday World* who she believes set him up for murder.

A tearful Jacqueline Conroy, the thirty-eight-year-old mother of the couple's four children, invited us into her stylish bungalow home at Laurelgrove, South Belfast.

In tears, she relived the spine-chilling seconds nine days ago when a pair of bare-faced killers shot her lover dead in broad daylight in Stephen Street in Belfast city centre.

And she told us: 'I don't care if it was the Provos who killed Daly.

'And I don't care if you publishing this gets me killed.

'But I believe that one of his close acquaintances set him up for murder.'

She went on to name who she suspects. But we cannot print the name for legal reasons.

The headline on the double-page spread inside ran: 'MUM STOLE FOR THE HIGH LIFE WITH DRUG DEALER KILLER'. The sub-headline said: 'Daly's lover says he was no godfather'. And the main story read:

The grieving partner of Provo murder victim Paul Daly invited *Sunday World* into her home yesterday — even though last weekend we described Daly on our front page as a drugs 'Godfather' and a killer himself.

Tearful Jacqueline Conroy, Daly's partner and the mother of four of his young children:

- DENIED that her executed lover was a drugs dealer.
- DENIED that he had murdered Gerard McKay by forcing him to swallow ten E tabs dissolved in Evian water at a flat on Belfast's Ormeau Road.
- CONFESSED that she herself was a criminal who shoplifted and stole to keep her family in opulent style.
- And ACCUSED an accomplice of Paul Daly's of setting him up for the barefaced IRA killers who gunned him down in cold blood in front of her.

We can't identify the man she accused for legal reasons.

We can reveal that security force sources still insist that Daly, thirty-eight when he was gunned down while picking his wife and one of his children up at Stephen Street in Belfast city centre in broad daylight just nine days ago, was a major drugs 'player'.

And 'though Jacqueline Conroy wants to meet the father of an E tab victim face-to-face to tell him her common-law husband didn't murder his boy, Gerard Jnr, Gerry McKay Snr still believes Daly killed his twenty-three-year-old lorry driver son.

Mr McKay said last night: 'I still believe Paul Daly murdered my innocent son.

'But I won't be meeting this girl.'

Jacqueline Conroy claimed there were drugs in the fatal flat where Gerard McKay died at 400 Ormeau Road on a night in late November 1998.

But she claimed they didn't belong to Daly.

Jacqueline Conroy was in the passenger seat of the small courtesy car Paul Daly had driven into Stephen Street to collect his wife and child.

She threw herself out the passenger side door as the gunmen struck.

Paul Daly tried to clamber out after her. But he was shot dead.

Police are still hunting his killers.

Jacqueline Conroy still finds it very difficult to talk about the bloody slaying.

The gunmen weren't wearing masks.

Asked if she knew them, she said: 'They wouldn't send anybody I knew to do that.'

She said if she knew them she would name them.

Asked if she believed the Provos carried out the execution, she said she didn't know.

Told that our sources — who had tipped us off about three previous IRA attempts on Daly's life — say it was, she replied that she thought one of Daly's accomplices had set him up for murder.

She named one man who, she said, had accused Daly before his death of setting him up for a drugs raid by the RUC when over £100,000 worth of drugs were seized.

We can't name him, either, for legal reasons.

But she was insistent that Daly was not a drugs 'Godfather', nor a big-time dealer, as she sat in the luxury bungalow which was on the market recently with an asking price of around £140,000.

She said the family — one of the kids is at a private school — had planned to move house, to the stockbroker belt of Cultra, North Down, at the end of this month.

She said she and Daly could afford the lifestyle they lived — he drove a Range Rover jeep, the room where we sat on expensive leather furniture was floored with antique pine — because, in a shock confession, she admitted:

'I am a thief.

'I went out and stole when we needed money.

'There just wasn't any money in drugs.

'I am a shoplifter. This might get me jail. But I don't care.

'I want to put the record straight.

'We had a house in North Belfast which appreciated very quickly in value. We sold it and made quite a bit of money.

'That's how we were able to live here.

'But everything you see in this house was got with my money,' Jacqueline Conroy said.

'I went out and shoplifted, stole clothes, and then sold them on to others.

'When my father, a decent man from County Tyrone, reads this, I will be in big trouble.

'But what do I have to lose now that Daly has gone?'

Strangely, throughout the almost hour-long interview, she called her deceased common-law husband by his surname ... 'Daly did this, Daly didn't do that.'

And she denied bar-talk bouncing around Belfast that Paul Daly had left her a fortune of half a million in money salted away and bought in insurance policies because, after previous Provo attempts on his life, he knew they were eventually going to catch up with him.

Jacqueline Conroy said there was only one insurance policy to cover the mortgage in the event of Daly's death, and another policy which would leave around £50,000.

Last week, two of Daly's ex-accomplices offered us still photographs of the murdered 'Godfather'.

They wanted £20,000 for the pictures. Of course, we refused.

But last night Jacqueline Conroy pleaded with us: 'Please don't pay money to any scum like that for pictures of Daly. I'll give you any you want.'

She did. And they are published on these two pages and on the front page.

And there was a second, shorter story on that double-page spread. Jacqueline Conroy had remained true to her word that she would give us pictures of Daly as I hadn't paid any money to the two men who wanted to sell his pictures the previous Saturday.

When I re-emphasised to her that I hadn't, wouldn't, and had no intention of doing so, she pulled out an old biscuit tin full of pictures from behind the arm of the settee she was sitting on. She placed them on a coffee table. And she said: 'Take what you want.'

I asked her would she pose for a picture. She said she would. I summoned Conor in, and he started snapping. It was almost surreal. The paper had gone after Daly, relentlessly, wanting him brought to justice — for Gerry McKay's sake, and the sake of his murdered son. And here we were, in the house Daly had lived in, with his partner, offering us any pictures of him we wanted.

As it turned out, we used a picture of him when he was younger, posing Rambo-style in army fatigues, with a replica Armalite rifle in his hands, on the front page. Inside we used four more pictures of him, and one of a tearful Jacqueline, across the spread.

Underneath one of Daly posing in a pair of skimpy swim-pants in the sun, and built like a brick shithouse with his champion weight-lifter's frame, we ran the third story. The headline ran: 'THUG WAS TOUGH NUT'. The story read:

Paul Daly always fancied himself as a 'hard man.

These pictures prove it — whether showing off his weight-lifting champ's body, or posing in mock army combat fatigues with replica guns ... still stripped to the waist.

And he walked out of court with just a suspended sentence recently after beating another bodybuilder so badly he put him in intensive care.

But large chunks of his life — and death — were dogged by bad luck.

During his funeral last week, for instance, relatives who were among the small cortege of under fifty mourners returned home ... to find that their house had been burgled and trashed.

And Daly's son from a previous relationship jumped the compassionate parole he was granted for his father's funeral to go on the run.

There were reports Paul Daly had vowed to avenge his father's death.

But his dash for freedom ended at 3 a.m. on Friday morning, when police picked him up on Belfast's Antrim Road.

He is now back behind bars.

Still, the latest Provo death squad shooting of Daly has sent others on the run.

. Some of the top drugs 'Godfathers' in Belfast and elsewhere are now living in fear for their lives.

And *Sunday World* sources have told us of two more men who are on a DAAD (Direct Action Against Drugs) deathlist.

They are now on the run and in hiding, too.

We said our goodbyes and left. The neighbours in the smart suburban avenue gave us strange looks. Until his murder, they seemed to have little idea of who was living next to, or near them.

For Conor and I it was an eerie feeling. There was a kid's toy truck, one of the pedal jobs, abandoned on the front lawn of the house. It obviously belonged to one of the Daly kids. You couldn't help but feel sorry for them. After all, they'd lost their 'Da'. But then again, as they grow up, how many more Paul Dalys are there going to be lurking out there in the undergrowth of life, waiting to poison kids like them — with drugs?

And as we left, pictures, as promised, in hand, Jacqueline Conroy's last words to us were: 'And don't forget, if those scumbags come back offering you pictures of Daly ... don't pay them one shilling, not a brown penny. You promised.'

Yes.

We were never going to. And, now, we didn't need to.

The Sequel: Part 4

'Did she talk about me? Did she mention my name?'

It was five hours after I'd met Jacqueline Conroy. We'd gone 'next door' to the pub beside the office, the Duke of York, to get a bite to eat and have a pint. A punter bounced in, literally. He was as jumpy as a leprechaun in a bed of nettles — all over the place. He walked past me once. Went to the toilet. Then came back.

He said: 'You know me.'

I bluffed my way. I didn't. He then told me his name. (I am not disclosing it here, for reasons that will become obvious).

He then asked me: 'Did Daly's woman talk about me, mention my name, when you talked to her this morning?'

Now, how the hell he knew I'd been up and talked to Jacqueline Conroy is beyond me, but the bush telegraph among drugs dealers and their cohorts is acute, and cute.

Anyway, I told him she had. I told him she said, upfront and unafraid, that she thought he had set Daly up for the Provos' hit squad. The reason, she said, was that this boy was 'shooting his mouth off' that he was going to 'have Daly done', because he believed Daly had set him up for an RUC Drugs Squad raid when he lost over £100,000 in drugs.

He denied that point-blank. He said it was the other way around, that Daly had been threatening to kill him if he caught up with him.

However, this boy told me other things that could, undoubtedly, cost him his life if recorded here.

He quickly slugged down one pint. He was obviously in an agitated state. But I wanted to know more. I put a pint up for him. His mobile phone went. He went outside to answer it. The pint was still sitting there an hour later. He never came back.

But during the brief, almost whispered bar room conversation, he claimed that the Provos had tried to shoot *him* dead *three times* the previous day, on Friday 11 May.

On Sunday, 20 May, eight days after that pub meeting, we ran another follow-up story to the Daly killing. It revealed that the Provos still had a 'hit-list' of another four drugs dealers on their 'wanted' list. The man who had come to see me in the pub was, as it transpired, on it.

The front page story published on 20 May read:

'Ulster's drugs war could spark another terror war.

The *Sunday World* has learned of an IRA death-list in their renewed purge of drugs dealers.

And one of the targets at the top of the list is the main supplier to LVF and UFF dealers.

He's also a Protestant with close links to both loyalist paramilitary organisations.

We have been told of four drugs dealers the Provos have in their sights following the gunning down of top target Paul Daly in Belfast just over a fortnight ago.

One of them told us last week: 'The Provos have tried to shoot me three times — in one day.'

But security sources believe if the main supplier to loyalist paramilitary drugs dealers is 'taken' out by the IRA — that could lead to bloody revenge and the possibility of a new terror war.'

The main story inside read:

A drugs dealer told us last week: 'The Provos tried to shoot me – *three* times in *one* day!'

He is one of four dealers understood to be on an IRA hit-list in their latest purge of alleged drugs dealers.

First, they murdered Cricky O'Kane in Derry.

Then they gunned down Paul Daly in broad daylight in front of his wife and child in Belfast.

Daly's partner, Jacqueline Conroy, claimed in the *Sunday World* last week that the weight-lifting father-of-four was not a drugs 'Godfather.'

The Provos have also shot and wounded a string of alleged dealers in what is thought to be a propaganda exercise in the run-up to the elections on 7 June.

One security force source said: 'The Provos are really putting themselves upfront again as the so-called 'people's police.'

And there has been an outcry recently in nationalist and republican areas about the upsurge in drugs dealing.

Certain newspapers which circulate in those areas have seen a significant increase on their letters pages from people complaining about the drugs epidemic.

And there is little sympathy on the ground when drugs dealers are murdered or maimed in shootings.

However, we have been told by our sources that four more drugs dealers have been pinpointed by the IRA for assassination.

They include one dealer who has been known to live recently in a house in the Malone Road stockbroker belt of Belfast.

Believed to be now aware of the assassination threat, he is understood to be 'moving between addresses'.

Another is a drugs dealer who once had a close 'working relationship' with the ex-porn queen turned drugs 'Godmother', Nuèla Fitchie.

She died in a police cell in Blackpool, England, after swallowing a package of drugs.

She had been arrested after a fracas in a hotel in England: a row which erupted while, it was alleged, she was setting up another lucrative drugs deal.

Fitchie — who used the stage name 'Luella' when she was performing live sex acts on stage — was deeply involved in the murder of small-time drugs dealer Thomas 'Tucker' Lockhard.

He was tortured, and his mutilated body dumped on the border.

One of Fitchie's main drugs business cohorts at that time later denied to *Sunday World* that he was involved in the Lockhard killing.

But he is now said to be on the Provo hit-list, too.

Another man on that 'death list' was named by Paul Daly's partner Jacqueline Conroy to us in an interview last weekend.

She gave us the name of a man she believed had 'set up' thirty-eight-year-old Daly for the deadly ambush in Belfast's Stephen Street.

She said he believed that Daly had double-crossed him on a drugs deal.

She said this individual believed Daly had tipped off police about a haul of drugs he had worth over £100,000, and that the drugs had been seized.

She said at the time: 'He was running about town before Daly's murder saying he was going to get him shot.'

Now, we understand, that drugs dealer is one of the four names on the Provo 'death list.'

But the most sinister development is that the fourth man on the alleged 'death list' is known to supply dealers in both the ranks of the Loyalist Volunteer Force and the UFF.

He runs a chain-link drugs importing network which stretches from the Continent — Spain and Amsterdam — into Dublin, and from there to the LVF stronghold of Portadown, and then on up to UFF dealers in Belfast.

His henchmen smuggle the drugs in on trucks owned by a major haulage firm.

But the way the drugs are hidden — in washing machines, TVs, catering equipment or whatever, which all have legitimate import accreditation — the bosses of the firm, or the drivers, are unaware of what is going on.

The same dealer was also involved in a botched drugs operation in County Antrim.

Police swooped and seized a consignment of drugs.

However, if the IRA 'take out' the main LVF/UFF supplier, that could spark retaliation from either, or both, organisations.

Said one senior loyalist source: 'It could well plunge us back into a new terror war.'

So far, the IRA have not claimed either the O'Kane or Daly murders.

And it is unlikely that the name their gunmen formerly operated under, DAAD (Direct Action Against Drugs), will surface again this time, given the hyper-sensitive political climate surrounding Sinn Féin's continued participation in the Assembly and Executive, and with the elections looming.

Plus, so-called 'clean' guns — weapons which have not been used in other Provo operations — could have been used for those two murders, and other so-called 'punishment shootings'.

So far, there have been no forensic findings forthcoming on the gun, or guns, used to murder Daly, for instance, and that is puzzling some politicians who believe that ballistics analysis could give an obvious clue as to who carried out the murder.

Another theory is that the gun, or guns, used to kill Paul Daly and in other shootings could indeed have been 'clean' weapons, used for the first time after having been smuggled in by Conor Claxton and his gun-running gang, now behind bars in Florida.

However, the result of the latest Provo purge is that many drugs dealers who believe they may be on a 'death list' are on the run.

Said one underworld drugs source: 'There are a lot of boys keeping their heads down. If the Provos can take out a hard man like Paul Daly with seeming impugnity — they can take out anybody.'

And the moral of this whole 'VICTIM' chapter, from start, through the sequels, to finish?

The moral is that the drugs 'Godfathers', and their executioners, have no morals.

Especially when it comes to the murder, still unsolved, of young men like Gerard McKay Junior — sent to his grave at the tender young age of just twenty-three — leaving his father, Gerry, still seeking the real truth of what went on in his son's flat way back in November 1998.

10

Nuèla 'Luella' Fitchie — The Godmother

'Dear Tucker,

When you get this I hope you have had a good break and your head is sorted. I have missed you and worried about you that much that I've been clean now for, well, since the last night you and I had a bash. So I'm off to see wee Graeme for Easter but the 0411 is back on the air. Please let me know your [sic] OK. The heat is off over the water so let's let the rest die down then you and I can go back to work. I'm always your friend and love you lots.

Nuèla'.

Touching, isn't it? She even put a French-style 'grave' over the 'e' in her name. It was a letter she sent to low-level drugs courier Thomas 'Tucker' Lockhard. The reference to the 0411 being 'back on the air' was, of course, her mobile phone: a vital accessory to any self-respecting drugs 'Godfather'. In this case, however, it was Ulster's first drugs 'Godmother' who was back on the air.

118

She would later use that mobile phone to summon Tucker Lockhard to a meeting with her — where she dialled 'M' for Murder. Tucker's murder. That was after she had him tortured, interrogated, beaten to a pulp, stabbed, lacerated, mutilated, and then had his body dumped on the border — to try to make it look like his callous killing had been a terrorist murder. So much for the final line in the letter from the 'Godmother' to the hapless and doomed Tucker: 'I'm always your friend and love you lots'. We were given a copy of the letter later, by a 'sickened' friend of Tucker Lockhard after he died.

And the 'crime' that cost Tucker Lockhard his life. He allegedly double-crossed the drugs 'Godmother' by stealing E tabs he was smuggling in from Scotland for her, hidden in a secret dashboard compartment of a car on an Irish Sea ferry. He claimed he lost them. She didn't believe him. She summoned a team of 'heavies' to a flat in the 'Bible Belt' capital of Ballymena. They tried to beat 'the truth' — in other words, what they wanted to hear — out of their hapless kangaroo court victim.

She then ordered him executed after her gang pummelled him to a bloody and bruised pulp.

Friends of his say his face was almost unrecognisable. One source told us that so savage was his torture and death, that he could only be identified, eventually, in the morgue, by a signet ring given to him by his father, and which he wore on the 'pinky', or little finger, of his right hand. His body had been dumped naked, except for a pair of boxer shorts.

The manner of his death disgusted even the hardened criminals and ex-terrorists who were by that stage plying the drugs trade in Ulster. Known drugs dealers rushed to deny involvement in the obscene murder. One of them demanded an urgent meeting with two of our reporters in the first-floor bar of the Europa Hotel in Belfast on the Saturday morning before we were due to front-page the story of Tucker Lockhard's killing in the next day's newspaper. He thought we were going to implicate him. He was wrong, though we didn't tell him that at the time. But he had known Tucker Lockhard in his short, drugs-couriering life. And his attitude to the story we were running showed how cheap life is on the street among the drugs Mafia. He didn't give a fiddler's damn about Tucker Lockhard or Nuèla Fitchie. He only cared about himself. Barefacedly, he told us: 'I'm from a republican area, a republican background. If certain people find out that I've been consorting with Nuèla Fitchie, given her loyalist past and at one time living with the fella she did, I'm away for my tea.' 'Away for my tea' is a Belfast euphemism for getting 'dundered', shot dead, maybe even tortured and dumped almost naked, and almost unrecognisable, save for the signet ring, like Tucker Lockhard.

There are those who say that as Nuèla watched the torture and heard the anguished screams, moans, groans and pleas for mercy, she almost got as much pleasure out of that throwback to a scene from the Spanish Inquisition as she did from her previous 'career'.

For drugs 'Godmother' Nuèla Fitchie had once been a porn queen whose star turn was performing live sex on stage with punters packed into sleazy pubs and clubs throughout Ulster.

She had been an early developer. Even as a teenager, she was a tearaway, running away from home, while still a schoolgirl, to live with a much older man. One veteran cop remembers going to the flat at the behest of her parents (who were decent people from an ultra-loyalist area; her father was an ex-military officer) to order her home, and caution her sugar-daddy that he could face charges of, among other things, unlawful carnal knowledge of a girl under sixteen. Still stunned to this day by what confronted him, he recalls: 'She was brazen even then. But even though she knew it was uniformed policemen at the door of the flat, and even though she was only fourteen, she came to the door stark naked!'

She didn't go home to her parents then. And it wasn't long after that that she fell into the clutches of a man who was going to show her how to make money for herself — and for him. 'She was a natural beauty,' says her ex-manager (not the first man to put her on the streets, or on the stage). 'She could have been a page 3 model,' he says wistfully. 'Instead she chose porn.'

She became infamous on the pub and club circuits of Ulster. She was seldom out of the headlines in the more racy tabloid newspapers for her sexploits on stage. She would douse herself in baby oil to shine up her skin, tanned from lying on sunbeds, for those lewd shows. And the lolly was good.

Said Nuèla's ex-manager: 'In those days of the kinky sex shows, she changed her name: but only slightly. Her stage name was Luella. She thought that was more exotic. Typical of her. Though to the hordes of men she performed in front of — and often performed with, live on stage — she was exotic enough already. And she wasn't particular about where she performed. Remember, in those days, there were an awful lot of squaddies, British soldiers, serving in Ulster. Such was the security situation at the time, they went out on patrol, but were then confined to barracks. Almost all of Ulster was a "red alert" meaning no-go, area for them in those days. So they were confined to barracks. They had what were known as "plastic pubs" in the barracks in those days. They were made of plastic, but they were made to look like English "locals" back home for the lads on duty here.

'And it was in those pubs that the sex-starved squaddies were entertained — probably still are. Strippers were shipped over from places like London, Glasgow, Merseyside, Tyneside, to put on shows. And then there was Luella. I booked her into many of those barrack pubs. And the soldiers literally lapped her up — before the days when lap-dancing in clubs became the craze. She would perform live sex there. And she'd make a mint in tips — outside of the agreed fee, of course.

'She even performed *inside* the infamous Maze jail. The prison officers in there at one stage had organised a stag night for some bloke who was getting married. And Luella, to use her stage name, did the business that night. But just what kind of business she did I'm not prepared to go into,' said the ex-manager, who still wears flash suits and likes to play Jack-the-Lad around town. She earned big money for that.

But, according to associates, enough was never enough for Nuèla — on stage, or off it. She also wasn't averse to doing some 'charity' work. Said one source: 'She didn't only perform for prison officers. She was known to perform for loyalist prisoners, on occasion, too. They would come out of jail on weekend parole. They would be sex-starved. They wouldn't have much money. So she would give them — those she knew and liked, that is — a "good time" for free. That's why, among them, she was affectionately known not as a hard-hearted whore, but as "The Tart with the Heart".'

The 'hard-hearted' bit was to come later — when Nuèla delved deeper and deeper into drugs dealing. And the spin-off in money from that allowed her to stop selling her own body — and start selling other girls'. She went into partnerships, not least with a blonde bimbo called 'June the Balloon' McKibbin. She, Nuèla, and other male drugs dealer pimps set up brothels in

Belfast. They weren't down-at-heel whorehouses, either. They picked the best apartments in the plushest parts of town: like Cherryvalley, in the stockbroker belt of East Belfast.

'June the Balloon' McKibbin in particular certainly proved herself a worthy partner to Nuèla. The twenty-nine-year-old ran a busy, bustling, booming brothel in Cherryvalley. The blue-rinsed brigade of ladies out walking their dachshunds and poodles in their fur coats in Cherryvalley would have had on-the-spot coronaries if they had twigged to what was going on under their powder-puffed noses.

The plush apartment was less than a mile from the RUC's main operational headquarters for the whole of Ulster. It was called Roxanne's Escort Agency and McKibbin ran the plush brothel with one of Belfast's most brash criminals, Stephen 'Brunt' Smith.

The thirty-four-year-old, originally from the working-class Falls Road in Belfast, is, at the time of writing, on the run from the Garda Síochána in Dublin, after he and his drugs-running cohort Liam 'Fat Boy' Mooney were caught in Dublin with a massive cache of drugs. Another of their gang, Kevin 'Maxi' McAlorum, posted thousands of pounds in bail for them, but both 'Fat Boy' and 'Brunt' did a runner and fled the country. McAlorum went back to court in Dublin to ask for his bail money back. He was almost laughed at by the Judge.

But in the days when Smith was running the King's Manor brothel with McKibbin, he was laughing all the way to the bank. They had up to twenty 'escorts' working for them round-the-clock in both the Cherryvalley 'agency' and in another brothel close to Belfast's 'Jewel in the Crown' concert hall and conference centre, the Waterfront Hall on the banks of the River Lagan — a focus for many international businessmen and entertainers.

Said one of their 'girls': 'The punters are charged £80 for a half-hour sex sessions but June and Brunt take £30 out of that. The place goes non-stop and they are making a fortune.'

Plus, they were running a phone-in service — with prostitutes on offer, and on order, for clients who were staying as guests in some of Belfast's top hotels. One night-doorman was later to confess, on TV, that he worked hand-in-glove with McKibbin and Smith's sex-for-sale ring — for three years!

Smith was on a roll. Looking like a butter-wouldn't-melt-in-the-mouth schoolteacher when he wore his scholastic round-rimmed, wire-framed glasses, he was, in fact, a hardened criminal. He had spent time in jail for armed robberies. Friends say he had brains to burn. And he was brazen with it. That became apparent when he and his fellow scam mate Liam Mooney were reported at one stage to have pulled off a bare-faced and massive drugs 'sting' in Amsterdam — ripping off a Pakistani drugs supply gang for £1 million worth of cannabis in a daring back-door warehouse raid.

Meanwhile, Nuèla was coining it, enough for her and her blonde bimbo friend 'June the Balloon' to afford long and luxurious holidays in the sun: either in Spain, Tenerife or South Africa, where, it was reported, she had accumulated enough capital to have business interests in Sun City.

However, there was trouble in paradise. That was when 'June the Balloon' and her partner in crime Smith ran into a 'sting' of the wrong kind themselves. They were rumbled by an investigative BBC Northern Ireland TV reporting team. Reporter Andy Davis, posing as a businessman in search of sex, bluffed his way into the Roxanne's apartment HQ and taped secret film footage for the award-winning 'Spotlight' current affairs programme. He even bargained with McKibbin for a price to bring some of his bogus business colleagues to do business with the 'escorts'. McKibbin, using the cover name 'Denise', arranged to meet the reporter in the Stormont Hotel, not far from King's Manor, to continue discussions. But she insisted on bringing her business partner 'Brunt' Smith.

The meeting never took place. Smith, who had by now abandoned his girlfriend and baby to live with McKibbin, smelt a rat. But the BBC programme still went out — and McKibbin was branded 'Madame Sin'. It took only days after that for the brothel business in plush Cherryvalley to go up in smoke, too.

But that wasn't the only thing that threatened to go 'up in smoke' when Smith, or 'June the Balloon' were around. At one time, *Sunday World* reporter Hugh Jordan was hounding them relentlessly in print. He drove a red Mercedes car. Smith and McKibbin planned to lure him to a meeting in the King's Head pub, opposite the world-famous King's Hall boxing arena on the Lisburn Road in South Belfast. And, while they kept Jordan in the pub talking, they planned to have his Merc torched outside in the car park! Hugh, as usual, had contacts who kept him right, and he was tipped off about the plan. The reporter, in turn, tipped off the police. There was going to be another 'sting' operation, but this time it was going to be Smith's would-be arsonists who would be 'stung' — by undercover police. However, again, Brunt Smith welched on the meeting.

There was a further threat of retribution by fire. The police once warned me that because of our campaign against drugs dealers, 'Fat Boy' Mooney and Brunt Smith in particular, the dealers planned to buy an apartment close to my home. A very senior RUC source told me that they were going to use that apartment as a 'sleeper' — no one staying in it, just for one purpose. And that purpose was to store petrol. 'Then, in the dead of night,' the police source warned me, 'they are going to splash petrol all round your house. They are then going to petrol bomb it.' I asked the senior police officer had he any idea when they planned to do it. The reply was stark and stunning. 'When you, your wife, and your family are in it,' he said. Fortunately, the police, through informers — the drugs scene is littered with them — had rumbled the petrol bomb plot. Smith and Mooney were spooked, and backed off. But with apartments going for over £100,000 in that vicinity at the time, it showed that money — or morals — were no object to the likes of callous criminals like Mooney and Smith.

Nuèla had, by this stage, taken up living with a 'main player', a UVF commander later to be involved in a major loyalist arms-smuggling scam in South Africa. But the UVF were to turn on her when she turned to drugs. At one stage, she approached the *Sunday World* with the story that the UVF were asking her to pay them thousands of pounds to allow her to continue the pursuit of her growing drugs empire.

Some of the stuff was believed to be coming from West Indian 'Yardie' gangs who, with a string of drugs-related gun killings in Britain, were proving they could be as ruthless as the paramilitaries back in Ulster.

The day before she died, Nuèla and others had travelled to England for a meeting. There was an argument in a hotel. Nuèla is said to have produced a knife at one stage. The police were called. She was arrested, reportedly drunk, aggressive and abusive. She was put in a cell in a Blackpool police station. It had apparently been decided, as is the policy in some police forces, to let her 'sleep off' the drink before being questioned and maybe charged in the morning.

Nuèla was not to see the next dawn. Fearful of a police search the next morning, she swallowed a plastic packet of E tabs, whole. Even worse, when they at first passed through her system, she is said to have swallowed them, again. She was found dead in her cell.

Tragic, said some. Poetic justice, said others, noting sombrely that those who live by the E tab ... well, you know the rest.

But there was another bitter and ironic twist to the death of Nuèla Fitchie in that Blackpool police cell. That was the size of the plastic bag of E tabs which she swallowed, twice, and which proved fatal. It was the same type of bag, although not with as many Es in it, that, sources say, was in the consignment that she accused Tucker Lockhard of stealing from her. 'Maybe,' said a friend of Tucker Lockhard's after the porn-queen-turned-drugs Godmother's death, 'maybe, just maybe, there is a God after all ...'

Nuèla Fitchie was buried in her father's grave in a neat little cemetery near her upmarket home in Ballyclare, County Antrim. The house was in one of those pseudo-English new-builds, called Huntingdale. While she was still in her coffin, even before her funeral, a cold-hearted thief stole her Porsche! He was one of her ex-lovers. Nuèla had acquired the top-of-the-range Porsche as a 'wee reward' for her dual drugs and porn queen lifestyle. It was the pride of her life, even more a stamp of 'class' than the Huntingdale home. But she made the mistake of taking the Porsche to Belfast airport before she made her ill-fated, and final, drugs-buying sortie to England. And when she died in that Blackpool police cell, an ex-lover then living in England jetted back to Belfast and stole the Porsche. He drove it onto an Irish Sea car ferry and back to England. One source said later: 'Nuèla may have owed him money. It was payback time for him. But it was a cold-hearted move. The bastard didn't even stick around for her funeral ...'

As it was, Nuèla took many secrets to the grave with her — not least her part in the murder of Tommy 'Tucker' Lockhard. But perhaps one of the biggest secrets concerns a big-time British sports star. Reports have persisted since her death that there is a picture of Nuèla with him. She is riding a horse naked, Lady Godiva-style. He is leading the horse by the reins. That picture has never appeared in the public domain. But perhaps, unlike the Porsche, Nuèla took it to the grave, in her coffin, with her ...

11

Firebombed!

'Jimmy, where are you?'

'I'm at home, Chris. I've just got out of a taxi.'

'Well, get back into it and get back into town quick — your office is on fire!'

The telephone call to my home just after midnight on Thursday, 21 January 1999, was from my mate, Chris Moore, an award-winning TV journalist who, almost single-handedly, was responsible for bringing down the Dublin government of the then Taoiseach Albert Reynolds over the Father Brendan Smyth paedophile priest affair. I had been out with my wife celebrating our wedding anniversary — two days early. The anniversary is on 23 January. But that year, that day was a Saturday. And Saturdays, on Sunday papers, mean work, from early morning until late at night. So the wee celebration was two nights previously. We had just arrived home with some friends when Chris rang.

A businessman running a commercial print house opposite our *Sunday World* office had been burning the midnight oil to meet an urgent contract. It was just as well. He heard a huge fireball explode in the foyer of our office. We were on the ground floor of a three-storey block. When he looked out, he could see flames shooting right up the stairwell, and smoke billowing out through the main door. He first phoned the fire brigade. They rushed to the scene. He wanted to phone me, but he didn't have my number. He knew Chris, and so phoned him, and Chris phoned me.

I jumped straight back into the taxi. And when I got to our office, the foyer and stairwell were a mess. A crowd had gathered in the street. Most of them were from the pub next door to our office — the Duke of York, our 'local'. The firemen had just finished dousing the flames. But the stench and the flame and water damage, even in the dead of night, were all too evident. Thankfully, the fire doors on all the offices, including the premises above us, had done their job.

The arsonists trying to silence us for our campaign against the drugs 'Godfathers' had tried to burn us out. They failed. When I asked a fireman to kick open the door to our own office — the locks had melted in the heat — I was relieved to see that all of our computers and files and records and back copies of the paper were unscathed.

On morning TV and right through the next day, myself and the entire *Sunday World* team in Belfast, and in Dublin, sent out a message to the firebombers who had tried to silence and burn us out. It was to become our motto: 'We're not beat yet! We are *not* stepping back.'

Meanwhile, the big question immediately after the fire was: '*Who* had tried to burn and put us out of business?' We didn't have far to look. By the following Sunday, three days after the firebomb blitz on our office, we were pointing the finger at one man: Brendan 'Speedy' Fegan, at that stage still alive. (He was gunned down by the Provos several months later.)

As already revealed in the murder saga surrounding Frankie Turley (see Chapter 7), Fegan was no stranger to Wild West-style 'bounties'. He had put a price on Turley's head. That was in cash: £20,000. Now, it was our turn. This time he got it cheap. The two firebombers he hired already had a grudge against us. So the price they were prepared to take was just £500 worth of Ecstasy tablets each, known at the time as 'Mitsubishis' — to torch our office.

One of them was the brother of a drugs 'Godfather' we had been hounding. He was running a drugs network on Ulster's so-called 'Golden Triangle', the seaside and tourist honey-pot centred on the world-famous Giant's Causeway. The 'Triangle' is formed by the seaside towns of Portrush and Portstewart, and then inland to the heavily student-populated town of Coleraine, where Northern Ireland's second biggest seat of learning, the University of Ulster, has its main complex. Thousands of young people would flock to the pubs and clubs there — and to well-organised raves — during the week and at weekends. They were supplied by dealers whose networks spanned both paramilitary involvement and gangs run by independent dealers.

One such 'independent' was the brother of one of the fire-bombers who targeted our office. At the time of writing, the arsonist is in jail after being convicted on drugs offences. However, he can't be named here, because he was never tried or convicted for the firebombing.

Suffice to say, we got our own back — if only in a small way. We discovered that he was getting drugs smuggled into the jail. We were also told the name of the person who was smuggling the small blocks of cannabis into him. We even discovered that the person smuggling the drugs in had also managed to get a fold-up knife in behind bars, so that our man, the firebomber, could cut up his cannabis. We blew the whistle on that little scam in the paper. And when the 'screws' staged a raid, they even found the smuggled-in cannabis-cutting knife hidden behind a radiator, taped to the wall.

So that particular firebomber wasn't as smart as he thought he was. And neither was his accomplice in crime the Thursday night they torched our office. The second felon was a known, small-time hood from the New Lodge district of North Belfast who was only starting out on the fringes of the drugs scene. And he wasn't full of 'the smarts', either. To this day, we can't prove it, but the forensic people told us later that the arsonist pair's modus operandi, from what they could later decipher, wasn't in the SAS class. Indeed, the forensic experts were prepared to bet that one, or both, of the firebombers didn't need a barber for a while, or mightn't have needed their eyebrows clipped, or even a shave. Because, as they told us after examining the scene, 'It looks like one, or both, of these boys could have been scorched, badly, by their own botched firebombing efforts.'

What happened was this. The two arsonists drove around past our offices two, maybe three times that night. They were driving a blue hatchback car. Unfortunately, although a couple of people noticed the vehicle, it was never captured on one of the closed-circuit television security cameras dotted around Belfast city centre (and, incidentally, now located on our outer office wall). Their MO was simple, and primitive. Usually when firebombers struck, they would have devices concealed in cassette or video tape boxes, which they would hide in stores or offices, and which would ignite after closing time. They couldn't do that with us. We wouldn't, obviously, let them in. So instead, they broke in through the main door of the building in the dead of night. They doused the floor and walls of the foyer and hall of the building with cans of petrol, which they'd obviously been carrying in the back of the hatchback — a car, we learned later, probably registered in Dundalk, close to Speedy Fegan's home town of Newry, on the border. They couldn't get into our actual ground floor complex, because it was locked and there was a special extra-security magnet-plate lock to stop gunmen or bombers getting in. So they poured their petrol. Then they struck a match. And *whoosh*. The petrol ignited. It did damage to the office foyer and stairwell all right.

But as the forensic expert explained the next day: 'If petrol is poured like that, a vapour "cloud" immediately builds up. And when a match is lit it's the vapour "cloud" that explodes into flame first. So either one, or both, of the comedians who tried to burn your office could well have burned his hair, eyebrows, moustache, beard, even the hairs on his chest, with it.' The next day, we had a drink to that. And we hoped the damage done to the firebombers was plural, not singular.

But what had put the notion of firebombing into Speedy's close-cropped head? The answer came from reporter Hugh Jordan. He discovered that two days before the attack on the *Sunday World* office, firebombers from a rival drugs gang had tried to launch a petrol bomb attack on Fegan himself. Except they got the *wrong* house. They targeted a house in Glengormley, a densely populated village-style community on the outskirts of North Belfast. The assailants smashed through a downstairs window with a hammer. They doused petrol around the downstairs room. And they tried to torch the whole house. But Fegan had moved out of the house shortly before. A young mum and her five kids were now living in the place. They were lucky to escape with their lives. And they fled the house afterwards, fearful of what happened. And fearful to live there after learning who had been the householder before them.

But, at least, there were some positives from the firebombing of our offices. The first was, of course, that no one was killed or injured, anywhere in the complex. The second was that no major damage was done, internally, to any of the offices in the complex. The third was that the whole ugly episode strengthened everyone's resolve to go on exposing and fighting the drugs dealers (see read-out of front-page editorial at end of this chapter).

And the fourth and fifth good things to come out of the whole aftermath of that literally burning issue?

The colourful and charismatic then Secretary of State, Mo Mowlam, had been one of the first on the phone to make sure we were all alright, to offer whatever help she could, and to then publicly condemn the firebombers. Plus, privately and typically, she called the arsonists a few colourful names, names that they were never baptised, but, seeing as we are a family newspaper, we never repeated them in the *Sunday World* ... and I am certainly not going to do so here, however justified they were! The following Thursday, a week after the firebombing, Mo's Press Attaché called. She said that the Secretary of State wanted to come down and visit the staff and office, to show her 'solidarity'. She asked if a visit on Saturday would be suitable.

I said that it would, but that I wouldn't be there. She asked me why not. I said: 'Come hell or high water, I'm going to the biggest match in the history of Ulster rugby.' (Well, we'd been through hell ... and we'd certainly had plenty of high water when the firemen put out the blaze!) The Press Attaché was somewhat taken aback. 'What's the match?' she asked.

'Ulster versus the French club Colomiers in the final of the European Cup at Lansdowne Road,' says I, adding: 'I'm surprised Mo isn't going to be there. Half of Ireland is. Including the Taoiseach Bertie Ahern, the President Mary McAleese, David

Trimble, Gerry Adams, John Hume …' and on and on.

There was a kind of gulp at the other end of the line, the kind of gulp you would have heard from the English when Ireland scored a last-minute try against them to clinch the match.

'Oh, we'll be back in a short while,' said the attaché.

Everyone else in Ireland had seemingly heard about the match. But someone, somewhere, had neglected to tell the Secretary of State at Stormont, who, admittedly, was up to her oxters in knife-edge political talks at the time. However, half an hour later, the call came back from Mo's eyrie at Stormont Castle. The Secretary of State would be going to the game. But she would still like to come to the office on the Saturday morning.

I said she was welcome, though I doubted if she could still make it to Dublin in time for the kick-off with the huge exodus that would be 'going down the road' from Ulster that day.

And I politely apologised that I still couldn't be in the Belfast office. I had four pages of 'colour', or features, to fill in the Northern edition of the paper on the invasion of Dublin by the tens of thousands of fans from the Red Hand Province. So I needed to be in Dublin for the 'colour' on the Friday night and the Saturday morning. And, with a busted snout, and two cauli-flower ears sitting like satellite dishes on the side of a baldy head bearing so much scar tissue it looks like a roadmap of Ireland — all a legacy of too many scrums, rucks and mauls in the game played by big men with odd-shaped balls — I had to be there for the craic, and the stout, and the singing, as well.

But Mo's Press Attaché said she would still be visiting the office in the morning, and heading for Dublin in a chopper in the afternoon, to be at the match on time.

Mo did visit the office on the Saturday morning, 30 January 1999, before being choppered down to the big game. The rest of the folk there gave her a good time: the plonk had been ordered in from the pub next door, and there were 'sarnies' and other finger-buffet refreshments. But Mo didn't forgive me for not being there. She picked up a piece of headed notepaper from my desk. She squiggled out the *Sunday World* heading and address. She superimposed, in her own handwriting, 'Stormont Castle'. And in a note that started 'Dear Jim', she said she had indeed been with the folks to show solidarity and to urge them to keep taking on the drugs barons. She wished us all the best in the future. And she signed off: 'Yours sincerely, Mo.'

But life was never that straightforward or simple with Marjorie 'Mo' Mowlam. Underneath, she penned an addendum. And it *was* simple and straightforward. Because I had 'pissed off' to Dublin, it read: 'P.S. Forget the Knighthood!' She was, of course, only kidding … I think!

So no Knighthood. But there was some consolation. I eventually clambered up into the stand, after filing columns of 'colour' copy on the Saturday, to be with my wife, my boys, the Caugheys, the Mackins, the McNutts, the mates, and half of Ulster — including Mo waving in the other stand — to cheer for, and shed a tear after, that famous victory.

Colomiers crumbled to a thumping 21–6 defeat, completely capitulating to Simon Mason, Jonnie Bell, 'The Humph' (David Humphreys) at out-half, Andy Matchett, big Gary Longwell, Andy Ward, and the rest of the 'Aughnacloys' (The Boys), in front of a raucous, chanting, singing, cheering, jubilant capacity crowd.

They came from all four Provinces to support and celebrate Ulster being the first Irish team to lift the European Cup. Lansdowne Road that day was not a rugby emporium. It was a volcanic eruption of voices sparked by a firebomb, a maelstrom, of emotion.

But that takes us back to where we started this chapter. Throughout that weekend, it was still impossible to forget the firebomb attack on our office. I was thinking about it on the road back up to Belfast on the Sunday morning. And then I stopped to get petrol at Newry, just over the border, and to lift a copy of that morning's Northern edition of the paper. My heart lifted when I saw it. There, in full colour emblazoned across the front page, was the immortal headline: 'SALUTE THE SONS OF ULSTER'. It was in reference to the rugby, of course. But in another way, I thought, it was also a salute ... to all the folk connected with the *Sunday World* who had kept going, and kept getting the papers out, even in the face of a wicked, if futile, firebomb attack. Just like the Ulster rugby team, they had refused to step back. And they never will.

---

* The firebombing of the office occurred on the night of Thursday, 21 January 1999. The following Sunday, we ran a page 1 editorial, signed by me, as Northern Editor. The headline ran:

'Firebomb will not stop the *Sunday World* working for you'.

The text ran:

'*We* never step back. The *Sunday World* is back on the news stands this morning. We won't be stopped in what we have to do as part of this community. We live in it. We are proud and privileged to serve *you*, the people who read us, in exposing those who would try to kill in, or corrupt, this community. Or, like the drugs dealers do, poison the kids of this country we live in.

That's why, in spite of the firebomb attack on our offices on

Thursday night, we are back on the streets again. We will continue to pursue our policy of the four Ps.

- We will continue to write about Paramilitaries.
- We will continue to expose drugs Pushers.
- We will continue to hunt down evil Paedophiles who prey on innocent children.
- And we will continue in the biggest quest of all for this country — to promote Peace.

That is why we are back on the streets this Sunday again. And that is why, inside, we name the top drugs 'Godfather' who ordered, and paid for (in E tabs) our office to be torched.

We will not step back …'

Underneath, was a tag-in panel highlighted in red. It read:

'EXPOSED — DRUG DEALER WHO TRIED TO SILENCE US: Pages 6&7'

Fegan, who sent the firebombers to torch the office, got the message. He never bothered us again — except for the confrontation in the street shortly before his death.

12

What Bible Belt?

'Please, I want you to expose what is going on in this town ... My daughter was on that TV programme about drugs the other night. She sat there and told a pack of lies. She explained how she had "beaten" the heroin habit. She talked about going through "cold turkey". She talked about having been "cured". But she walked out of that TV programme. She got £200 for the interview. And she shot it straight up her arm!'

The despairing words came from a desperate father. He had continually tried to save his daughter from the depths of a heroin hell she was sinking into. He had hounded her around the drugs haunts and filthy squats in the town where they lived, imploring her to return home, to give up drugs and what he called the 'loose living' that went with it. He knew that, at just twenty-one, and already a recidivist heroin addict — as portrayed in her TV interview — she had no hesitation in selling her body, swapping sex for a 'hit' or more money to feed her increasingly expensive habit. And he was pleading with us, as reporters, to go and expose what was going on in his home town.

And where is that town? Ballymena, County Antrim. The

capital of the 'Holy Roller' area of rural Ulster known as the Bible Belt.

The town used to be renowned for different things — its prime beef, herded in from the lush acres of rich County Antrim farmland stretching for miles around and beyond Ballymena; its rugby club, proud to the present day, which produced heroes like British and Irish Lions Willie John McBride and Syd Millar — household names in places as far flung as the rugby meccas of New Zealand, Australia and South Africa.

And it was renowned for its religious fervour. It is, after all, the heartland of Paisleyism — where the 'Big Man', the Reverend Ian Paisley, struts his stuff and unleashes his zeal as both fire-and-brimstone preacher and hell-for-leather politician.

But Ballymena is now famous for another phenomenon: the hard drugs epidemic sweeping the Bible-belt town. It is a problem on a staggering scale. And its growth rate is phenomenal. Plus, there is the fallout. As more and more addicts craved more and more drugs, crime spiralled — break-ins, muggings, pensioners assaulted and robbed, organised raids on lonely farmhouses: in short, a nightmare. And all of this in the hub of where people once prided themselves as living in the 'Bible Belt'. It is estimated that up to 2,000 people are regular heroin users, which makes Ballymena — in terms of the addicts per head of population — the drugs capital of Ireland, even outstripping, statistically, Dublin, which has its own huge problems in inner-city estates like Ballymun.

And it gets worse. For in this heroin hell, it's not only adults that are addicted. It's kids as young as just thirteen years of age, too. Many of them come from the rundown and dilapidated housing estates of Ballykeel and the Doury Road in the town. The loyalist paramilitaries, especially the UDA/UFF, are strong in there. And since the UDA/UFF moved into drugs, the drugs have moved into those estates. So youngsters, especially young girls, get involved, and then get hooked. And they, even at such a tender age, live their lives in hovels and drugs dens as hookers. The male dealers 'take up' with them — in other words, turn them almost into pubescent sex slaves — claim them as their own, and sleep and have sex with them. And for what? More drugs. It's a bleak picture. But the evidence is there.

Take the man who rang up talking about his daughter 'shooting up' her £200 interview fee as soon as she got out of the TV studio. He says: 'I know she's been sleeping around. It tortures me. I'm her father after all. I hate to see her doing this to herself. But I know, and can take you to, squats and flats where girls as young as thirteen and fourteen are doing exactly the same thing. These drugs "Godfathers" think they own them. They use them, and abuse them. I know. I have been round this town trying to pull my daughter out of heroin dens. I know the evil bastards who are selling this poison.'

And if further graphic evidence is needed of the hurricane of heroin now targeting Ballymena, the RUC in Belfast raided a house in the city's Kansas Avenue as this book was being written. They seized heroin with a street value of £1 million. And where did the police say it was headed for? Ballymena. A number of men were arrested in the huge drugs bust. They were later charged. At the time of writing, the case is *sub judice*. More details cannot be divulged.

But that heist, while a big success for the Drugs Squad, only presented more headaches for the police in Ballymena. Because it caused a shortage of heroin. When the price of heroin goes up, the addicts turn to crime to get money for their much-needed 'hits', and the crime rate rockets. It was the same when a major police undercover operation code-named Operation Patsy swooped and scooped ten drugs dealers in the town. That was in late 1999. The extensive operation was reckoned to have cost £6 million. But it led to a heroin famine for a while. And the prices went through the roof.

By February 2000, addicts in Ballymena needed £700 a week to feed their insatiable habits. They turned to crime to do it. And the remaining dealers cashed in, big-time. The 'Godfathers' who remained to ply their evil trade on the streets upped the ante: they were making £3,000 profit on each ounce of heroin. Some of them, replenishing supplies from wherever they could get the heroin — Liverpool, Amsterdam, across the border from Dublin — were shifting fifty ounces a week.

Said one addict of the exploding crime wave: 'My own grand-father was mugged by a heroin addict. I was ashamed. Days ear-lier, I had snatched an old lady's handbag to get money for the next hit. I'm not proud of what I did, but the addiction is so strong you would sell your own soul for a bag of heroin.'

And there was squalor. Young addicts could be found in 'squats' surrounded by filth, their own excrement and urine. And it was here that they were injecting heroin into their feet, because the veins in their arms had collapsed from over-abuse. It was also in such primitive surroundings that addicts who over-dosed were dumped, for better or for worse. Said one source in a filthy squat: 'If they wake up, they wake up. If they don't, they don't.' And there are rising numbers of addicts who don't wake up around Ulster.

Another town with a major problem is the seaside resort of Bangor, fourteen miles South of Belfast in County Down. A short train ride from Belfast, it used to be a favourite haunt of both young people and pensioners for day-trips. Now tracts of the once-pretty town are haunted by heroin addicts. By February 2001 community workers battling abuse calculated that there had been a dozen heroin-related deaths in the previous twelve-month period.

There had also been two terrorist-style murders — one a shooting, the other an under-car booby-trap bomb — linked to the drugs trade in the town. Both had occurred in the sprawling, loyalist-dominated Kilcooley housing estate, an 'overflow' project populated by many working-class families who had moved from Belfast. And the main doorman at a club who refused to allow the Loyalist Volunteer Force to ply drugs on the premises for which he was responsible was blown up in a van travelling in the town centre. Fortunately, although seriously injured, he survived.

However, in spite of brave bids to keep the lid on the burgeoning drugs trade in the seaside town, the problem is spiralling. At the time of writing, the price for a potentially lethal dose of heroin has hit rock bottom because of the overabundance of supply. A one-hit bag is known as a 'twist'. It could be bought for as little as £10. Contrast that with what was being asked in Ballymena a year before.

So serious had the problem become that Mark Gordon, a community worker specialising in countering drugs abuse with the Kilcooley Community Forum, believed that Bangor could well challenge Ballymena as the hard drugs capital of Ulster. He told reporter Steven Moore: 'Drugs in general have exploded in Bangor and North Down. I have figures for the amount of drugs seized in Bangor that you won't get from the RUC.' He claims that a recent haul of hundreds of thousands of pounds worth of heroin uncovered by police elsewhere in Ulster was bound for Bangor. And he says that in the months over Christmas 2000 —

the main partying season in the clubs and pubs — over £3 million worth of cannabis was seized.

He described the growth in the number of drug addicts as 'alarming'. He said a recent, official report suggested that there are between 250 and 300 heroin users in the North Down area. But he reckoned there could be four times that. He said that in the previous twelve months alone, the Addiction Team dovetailing into the Kilcooley Community Forum had listed one hundred new referrals.

But it wasn't only the use of drugs that was putting addicts in hospital. The 'godfathers' are well capable of doing that, too. Especially when addicts get drugs 'on tick' (on loan) and then can't borrow, beg or steal enough money to pay back the dealers. One addict, who wouldn't be named because he was terrified of the dealers exacting their own retribution on him again, told how he'd been 'tortured': 'They kidnapped me. They took me to a squat. They had a camping stove with a gas-flame cooking ring. They lit it. They stripped me, held me down over the stove, and scorched my genitals.' He said he found the money to pay them … after he left hospital.

Community worker Mark Gordon said he'd just visited a man in hospital recovering from a broken collarbone. He said that that injury, too, was the result of a severe beating from drugs dealers for non-payment of money owed. Gordon said the assaults and torture go unreported to police. 'People are too terrified to do that. They are afraid for their lives.' He also said that heroin addiction was not only gripping the unemployed as it strengthened its hold in Ulster. He said he knew many addicts 'who have secure jobs and are able to pay for their habit out of their wages'.

Community workers and academics are concerned that not enough is being done by the government and statutory agencies to deal with the spiralling drugs problems.

Agnes Smiley, whose son John died from a heroin overdose in August 1999, has since set up the Support Awareness Drugs Initiative. Her agency offers support for families of those on drugs — a legacy of heartbreak and hardship often overlooked when it comes to the aftermath of drug addiction. She says the centre she helps run is 'a place where friends and family concerned that a loved one is using drugs can come and get more information, and a sympathetic ear'. But both Mark Gordon and Agnes Smiley feel that they are working in a void when it comes to government recognition of the problem, or measures to help deal with it.

Academic Dr Karen McElrath, from Queen's University, is another who feels like she's hitting her head against a brick wall. She carried out an extensive report into heroin abuse in Northern Ireland that could have far-reaching consequences for anywhere with an addict population in Ireland — be it Dublin, Galway, Limerick or Cork. She is concerned about the side effects of heroin abuse: dirty shared needles and their potential to spread diseases such as HIV and Hepatitis B and C. Her report recommended, among other things, the provision of free needles for heroin addicts. And she wants a 'multiple sources' network to provide them, using chemist shops, needle exchange sites, drop-in centres like those pioneered in Bangor, hospitals, and street outreach programmes. The street initiatives, she feels, could help teach addicts how to inject as safely as possible, and show them how to clean their needles, if they don't have a supply of new ones.

And as for the dealers in potential death, it's one thing catching them and putting them behind bars, and quite another keeping them there. One week in February 2001 proved the point. The focus was back on the Bible Belt drugs capital of Ballymena. Drugs-busting Operation Patsy swept up a platoon of dealers there. A posse of ten were later jailed. One was John Dunlop, a convicted heroin dealer. He was incarcerated in the remote Magilligan jail in North County Derry. But in January 2001 he was allowed out on parole. He didn't return to the jail: he went on the run.

The episode proved so embarrassing that police chiefs resorted to posting his details on the Internet. They asked people to try to trace his whereabouts. The ploy worked. Over the weekend of 24–25 February, Dunlop was spotted in the housing estate drugs mecca of the Doury Road complex in Ballymena. The RUC got an address. They burst into a house looking for the fugitive twenty-three-year-old. They found him — hiding in the attic. But his original disappearance fuelled fears among politicians and the prison service about the number of inmates skipping while out on parole.

The fears were well founded. In the same week, on Thursday 1 March, the RUC swooped on a van in a loyalist zone of North Belfast. It was close to the Mount Vernon flats where just days previously a mini-arsenal of lethal pipe bombs and a bomb packed into a fire extinguisher were found. One thousand Ecstasy tablets were also uncovered in the makeshift bomb factory. The 3rd Battalion of the Ulster Volunteer Force is based in the Mount Vernon complex. This proved that they were into drugs — in spite of the UVF consistently trying to clean up any involvement it has in drugs-running.

The full details of the van find cannot be revealed here. By the time of this book going to press, the suspects detained may be the subjects of a court case, making the proceedings *sub judice*. Suffice to say that when detectives ran ID checks on the three suspects arrested, they discovered one was on the run from Magilligan jail. He, too, had skipped parole. He had been in for armed robbery. By the morning of 2 March, he was back behind bars again. The drugs — Ecstasy tablets and cannabis — were locked up, too, in the RUC's Drugs Squad headquarters on the Antrim Road in Belfast, not far from where the van was stopped. The street value of this haul was a whopping £1 million.

Nigel Dodds of the DUP has been the most outspoken in his party in the drugs war going on in Ulster. He is also a Member of the Legislative Assembly (MLA) at Stormont, and a Belfast City Councillor for North Belfast, where the massive drugs haul was seized. He urged police to investigate any paramilitary connection with the cache. And, significantly, he also called on the prison authorities to re-examine their policy on parole. Assemblyman Dodds said: 'Their whole attitude to home leave and how prisoners are treated gives no confidence to the ordinary citizen that crime is being punished.'

Mr Dodds knows all about being a target of crime. His young son, Andrew, died after fighting a brave battle against illness. But one night, before the wee boy died, the by now veteran DUP politician was visiting him in the Royal Victoria Hospital for Sick Children in Belfast. It was then that a heartless IRA assassination gang tried to murder Mr Dodds. Thankfully, their murder bid was thwarted.

Meanwhile, another father, this time in Ballymena, is fearful of his daughter dying. 'Bible Belt,' were the forlorn father's last words on that occasion. 'What Bible Belt?'

The Sequel
'TWENTY-SEVEN JUNKIE BABIES'

That was the headline splashed across the front page of the *Sunday World* Northern edition on 1 April 2001. But it was no April Fool joke. The front page write-off on the story, by News Editor Richard Sullivan, ran:

Babies are being born in Ballymena — addicted to heroin.

The *Sunday World* today reveals the full devastating effect of the killer drug on the capital of Ulster's Bible Belt.

For we can reveal that twenty-seven babies were born in Ballymena in the last eighteen months hooked on heroin.

Health officials failed to comment on the shock revelation but the figure was released to the *Sunday World* by shocked health workers.

The newborn children were put through a rigorous detox programme to wean them off the deadly drug.

The revelation comes in the wake of a £1.2 million Ecstasy seizure in the town this week.

The health workers had one figure. The health authorities, who had refused to comment when Sullivan put the claim to them in the first place, later issued a statement. They claimed the figure of twenty-seven babies born addicted to heroin in that eighteen-month period was wrong.

But they still declined to say exactly how many babies were born who needed detox treatment.

Six weeks later, another shocking and sad statistic emerged: that no less than eight people had died from heroin abuse in just six months.

The mantle of Ballymena being the 'drugs capital' of Ulster's Bible Belt was, tragically, living up to its name.

13

Johnny 'Mad Dog' Adair

'Don't call me "Mad Dog". That's what newspapers dubbed me. I don't want to be called that, anymore. I am now a community worker. I am not a drugs dealer.'

The words were those of Johnny Adair, dubbed 'Mad Dog' in newspapers, both broadsheet and tabloid, a long time before. Even before Adair, who became the boss of one of Ulster's most feared terror gangs, the Ulster Freedom Fighters, was jailed for sixteen years.

He, and two of his close allies, both paramilitary and political, had been with him when he called at the *Sunday World* office on a Monday morning not long after he got out of jail under licence — and before he went back in during the Shankill loyalist feud.

One of his co-callers was John White, once jailed for life for the brutal knife-slaying of a former nationalist politician, Paddy Wilson, a Senator in the old Stormont government, and his female companion, Irene Andrews. Both were kidnapped by a gang of loyalists as they left a Belfast pub on the summer's night of 24 June 1973. Ms Andrews was a Protestant, Paddy Wilson a Catholic. Wilson, also a Belfast Councillor and close friend of Lord (Gerry)

Fitt, was stabbed thirty-two times. He was also shot. Ms Andrews was stabbed nineteen times in what White's trial judge later called 'a frenzied attack, a psychotic outburst'. John White, on his release from prison, went into politics with the UDA/UFF's political wing, the Ulster Democratic Party. He subsequently represented the UDP at the white-knuckle negotiations at Stormont in the run-up to the signing of the Good Friday Agreement.

Adair's other co-caller was 'Winkie' Dodds, a longstanding 'heavy' and henchman of Adair's. And, with Adair back in jail, he still was helping, at the top, to look after Adair's 2nd Battalion 'C' Company UFF on the lower Shankill Road.

As it turned out, the trio had come to see me, but there were no reporters in the office that Monday morning. We normally work Tuesday-through-Saturday, being a Sunday paper. One columnist, however, that year's Entertainment Writer of the Year award-winner, Ivan Martin, was in doing his stuff early.

The next morning, a Tuesday, he told me what had happened. I immediately drove up the Shankill Road to Adair's HQ behind the security cage in the UFF prisoners' aid and advice centre, and rang the bell on the front gate. Johnny Adair, John White and 'Winkie' Dodds were there. I asked to see them. I was invited into the bleak backroom, with chairs sparsely placed around the walls of what seemed like a portacabin attached to the old and flaking front of the building. This, I was to find out later, was where the UFF chief usually conducted his interviews.

I asked them what the problem was. And I was stunned by its simplicity. Johnny Adair told me he no longer wanted to be dubbed 'Mad Dog' in newspapers. He said that as far as he was concerned, he was now out of jail and was carrying out community work. And that was what he wanted to be known as in future: a community worker.

Murdered Portadown, Co. Armagh businessman, Richard Jameson, with his wife and family, in a Christmas picture. Shortly afterwards, he was gunned down by LVF killers.

Richard's brother, Bobby Jameson, with a poster pillorying the LVF as pill pushers, after his brother's murder.

The squalor of a drugs den in the Bible Belt heroin capital of Ballymena, Co. Antrim.

John White, one of the 'main men' in the UFF/UDA/UDP set-up, centred around self-confessed director of terrorism, Johnny Adair.

The top gun in the IRA's gun-running ring in Florida: baby-faced Conor Claxton, later jailed in America.

Paddy Farrell, one of the first big-time Ulster drugs 'Godfathers', hid his racket behind a lucrative car sales business on the border. He had connections into the Dublin drugs cartels.

Blonde bombshell Lorraine Farrell — no relation to Paddy Farrell. But she was his mistress. Mystery still surrounds why both were found dead in the same bed in Drogheda, Co. Louth, killed by the same shotgun.

The good life: top drugs dealer and 'hard man', Edmund 'Big Edd' McCoy, reaps the ill-gotten gains of his illegal trade, jet-skiing in the Caribbean.

Al Capone, or 'Big Edd' McCoy? It's hard to tell from this gangster-style, gimme-the-good-life picture.

The face of evil — Hugh 'Cueball' Torney. He didn't threaten the author: instead, he said, he'd shoot one of his staff.

Frankie Turley had many narrow escapes in his life. But there was no way out when two gunmen eventually shot him from behind at a guns hide in County Antrim. It was Frankie who supplied the Sunday World with the limousine picture of Brendan 'Speedy' Fegan and Brendan 'Bap' Campbell.

Stone cold. That's Milltown murderer Michael Stone, even as he buttons up his bullet-proof vest. These days he's out from behind bars, but still a prime target for Republicans.

Cool dude drugs 'Godfather' Paul Daly, at the wheel of his white Merc. He was later to die at the wheel of a Peugeot 206 courtesy car.

The body of Paul Daly draped in a blanket where he was gunned down in Belfast, in front of his partner Jacqueline Conroy.

UFF boss Johnny Adair before the Secretary of State for Ulster, Peter Mandelson, ordered him back behind bars. This was the interview where — hands and arms raised — he expostulated: 'I'm no drugs dealer!'

Johnny Adair with a bullet sent to him through the post. This time it allegedly came from loyalists — before, he had been shot by republicans at a UB40 rock concert in Botanic Gardens, Belfast.

'Mad Dog' jailed

Belfast — Northern Ireland's most notorious Protestant militant was returned to prison on Friday for breaching his parole conditions, officials said. Johnny "Mad Dog" Adair, a former Ulster Defence Association commander, was sent back to prison after police arrested him at his west Belfast home. Revoking his early release from prison, Northern Ireland Secretary Paul Murphy said he believed Adair was a danger to the public. — A

12.1.03

Johnny Adair takes a dogged stance at Drumcree, Co. Armagh, surrounded by his T-shirt-wearing cronies and accompanied by his Alsatian, 'Rebel'. Even the dog wore a T-shirt bearing the motto of the Lower Shankill UFF.

It didn't quite work out like that, either with other newspapers 'bye-balling' the 'Mad Dog' nickname, or with other people, like the Secretary of State for Northern Ireland, Peter Mandelson, and RUC boss Ronnie Flanagan, accepting that Adair was merely engaged in community work.

But, at least, there was no threat from a self-confessed terrorist who had been threatened himself many times in the past — and who had escaped a fusillade of assassination bids.

On one occasion, a bullet ricocheted off a ring on his finger, as the gunman fired at his face, and Adair raised his hand to protect himself. Republicans had also tried to kill him with booby-trap car bombs. And failed. But the most notorious assassination attempt on Adair was to lead to one of the worst mass murders of the whole Troubles.

On the sunny Indian summer day of 23 October 1993, the IRA thought Adair was holding a 'Council of War' of UFF chiefs above a fish shop on Belfast's Shankill Road. They planned to 'take out' Adair and his terrorist elite in one go, by planting a bomb in the fish shop. The Provos claimed later that they did not mean to kill innocent people. IRA sources said the two young bombers, dressed in the white coats and little 'pork pie' hats worn by fishmongers, were meant to carry a huge Semtex device in a cardboard box into the shop. They were supposed to order the staff and customers out, place the bomb on the counter, and then let the timing device — set on a short fuse to catch Adair and his terror co-commanders still up the stairs, or coming down them — do the rest.

But the unthinkable happened. As one of the bombers — Thomas Begley, twenty-three, and later said to be educationally subnormal — placed the bomb on the counter, it exploded in his face. The fish shop was still packed with people. It collapsed like a pack of cards, leaving a smouldering mountain of bricks, mortar, roof tiles — and blasted, broken and bleeding bodies — on the ground. Ten people — men, women and children — died: bomber Begley among them. Another teenage bomber, Sean Kelly, was critically injured. (He was to recover, to be convicted, and handed down nine life sentences: but he, too, is now out of prison under the Good Friday Agreement 'amnesty'.) Over sixty innocent people were injured, many seriously.

But one intended murder bomb victim escaped unhurt, with not a hair on his head harmed. (And he had hair then: before the phase of the shaved, 'hardman' hallmark bald head.) He was Johnny Adair. And he wasn't in the building at the time of the bomb. Neither were his team of terror 'lieutenants'. The IRA had got it wrong. And created a mini-holocaust of innocent, Protestant people on the Shankill in their crazed craving to kill.

Adair was livid. Even more so when Gerry Adams, now the Sinn Féin president, carried the dead bomber's coffin — a gesture that stoked fiery political reaction worldwide. Adair wanted revenge for the Shankill bombing. He was so ruthless, he even drove into Catholic/nationalist areas wearing the soccer jersey of Glasgow Celtic football club. Many Catholics from Belfast and Derry support Celtic, even though their base is across the Irish Sea in Glasgow. There used to be a famous Belfast Celtic football club, but it was wound up. However, Celtic soccer shirts are commonplace in districts like the Falls Road and Andersonstown in West Belfast, and the Bogside in Derry. Johnny Adair's activities were mainly confined to Belfast. But he was known to go into Andersonstown and up the Falls, stalking potential targets, wearing a Celtic shirt as part of his disguise. He was actually a rabid supporter of the other, mainly Protestant partisan club in Scotland, Glasgow Rangers. Thus it was that Adair, later to confess that he was a self-styled 'director of terrorism', scouted out victims for his fanatical UFF gang.

It was for that 'director's' role that Adair was jailed for the first time.

RUC anti-terror squad detectives had literally hounded 'Mad Dog' during that directorship of his sectarian killer squads. Adair had been unable to hold his tongue. He boasted to policemen — on the beat, under the roof even of his own fortified homes — of what he and his UFF cohorts had done, and what they were capable of. What Adair didn't know was that the cops were 'wired', and he was being taped, recording dynamite and self-incriminating evidence. One of the those 'deep-throat' cops even looked up at the lampshade in Adair's house one night, police legend now has it, and said to Adair: 'Don't be talking so loudly, Johnny — the bulb up there is bugged.' And when the detective got back to his station, the Special Branch men went berserk. For they were listening in to his conversation with Adair ... and the eavesdropping 'bug' was indeed planted in the lampshade!

It was after escapades like that that Adair's confession came and he was put behind bars for sixteen years. But he was let out from the infamous Maze Prison, now closed, like squadrons of other convicted terrorists — loyalist and republican — under the 'early release' option of the Good Friday Agreement signed at Stormont in 1998. That Agreement was finally given the nod by the UDA/UFF and their political wing, the Ulster Democratic Party, before it was signed. But only after the then NI Secretary of State Mo Mowlam, in a hugely controversial political move, went into the Maze — known as Long Kesh during the IRA hunger strikes and dirty protests of 1981 — to talk to the UFF 'Commanders' behind bars. Adair was one of them.

Another was Michael Stone, who spoke to me about life in
the Maze at that time. He was the perpetrator of the 'Milltown
Massacre' when he attacked the funeral of the IRA's 'Gibraltar
Three' — the Provo trio who were shot dead by the SAS as they
tried to bomb British soldiers on 'The Rock'. Stone murdered
three mourners in his gun and grenade attack. He fled down the
steep hill in the Catholic graveyard at the top of Belfast's Falls
Road, pursued by furious funeral-goers dodging behind grave-
stones to escape flying bullets as Stone emptied one gun, then
started using another. He ran out of bullets. And, as he jumped
on to the hard shoulder of the Belfast–Dublin M1 motorway —
the motorway flanks the graveyard — he also ran out of steam.
His pursuers caught up with him. They were prepared to pummel
him to death — with their bare hands. But a police Land Rover
screamed to the scene. Armed riot cops rescued Stone. The furious mourners, however, got one of his guns. To this day, Stone,
since also released under the Good Friday Agreement amid a
blaze of worldwide publicity, believes that republicans will one
day exact retribution for the massacre at Milltown where the
IRA — with republican movement chiefs like Gerry Adams and
Martin McGuinness present — buried three of its 'martyrs' in
the cemetery's bleak, green-railed republican plot. And Stone
believes he will be shot dead: with his own gun — the same
weapon, its magazine empty, wrested from his grasp when the
crowd caught up with him on the M1 motorway.

So it was that when Mo Mowlam went to HMP Maze, both
Adair and Stone were among the waiting UDA/UFF entourage
there to greet her. The sight that also greeted her were men with
bulging biceps, sculpted shoulders, and thick thighs. The
Secretary of State could as easily have been visiting lifers in an
American jail. The loyalist UFF prisoners had adopted the US

long-term prisoners' discipline of 'pumping iron', and they were built like wannabe contenders for the Mr Universe competition. 'It was the macho-man thing taken to extremes,' recalls one prison officer. 'They would vie with each other to see who could get biggest, quickest.'

Michael Stone told me after he got out of jail: 'It was hard inside the prison. There were certain education projects we could lock into to get the time done. But bodybuilding and weightlifting became a passion. And for some it became an obsession.'

So much so, others recall, that drugs were even smuggled into the jail. Steroids. The drugs used for 'bulking up' by body builders. Stone maintains that he built a weight-lifter's physique by simply pumping iron, without any artificial aids or stimulants. He tells of Johnny Adair first entering the jail. He wasn't the 'Hulk' figure he soon became. Stone recalls: 'Johnny wasn't exactly a Colossus of Rhodes. He asked me to show him how to train properly to get a bodybuilder's physique. I agreed to do so.'

But other prisoners, and prison staff, were soon startled by the swiftness of Adair's progress into the ranks of behind-bars, pumping-iron titans. One source inside the jail at the time said prisoners were so desperate for steroids that even animal drugs were being smuggled in. One of these was the veterinary steroid, Clenbuterol. It is also known as 'Angel Dust'. It is used to artificially hasten the fattening of beef cattle for slaughter.

One ex-prison officer told us: 'We suspected Adair was taking the 'Angel Dust' to beef him up. He was the CO of the UFF prisoners from West Belfast, the Shankill,' the former warder said. 'In spite of that seemingly unified meeting involving all the jail UFF Commanders with Mo Mowlam, there were frictions and personality clashes between the various UFF factions. East

Belfast didn't particularly like the boys from the West, for instance. So, at the height of the 'Angel Dust' rumours, the East Belfast UFF didn't refer to Johnny as "Mad Dog". They called him "Mad Cow" — but only behind his back, of course.'

Meanwhile, before the floodgate releases of terrorist prisoners occurred after the 'amnesty' of the Good Friday Agreement, inmates jailed way back at the start of the Troubles in the late 1960s and early 1970s were getting out, having 'done their bird'.

There had been a loyalist paramilitary ceasefire in place since 13 October 1994, just six weeks after the Provos declared their first 'open-ended' truce, which came into effect at midnight on 31 August of the same year. Since the joint ceasefires — later breached by the Provos with their spectacular Canary Wharf bombing, but now back in place — or because of them, the RUC were able to clamp down on racketeering as never before. A special squad was even set up: code-named CI6, and based at Knocknagoney barracks in East Belfast.

The Provos had had the foresight to use their funds to get into legitimate 'front' businesses, buying pubs and taking over clubs, not only in Belfast and Derry, but in Dublin and Limerick, and, more importantly, in the dollar-rich and Irish/American hotbeds of New York and Boston. The IRA were later to move into smuggling — cigarettes, illicit booze — and running teams of 'bouncers' at selected pubs and nightclubs to provide not only subsistence for their ex-cons, but also, in the case of 'bouncers', jobs as well. Some of the most notorious Provo gunmen and bombers are now wearing bow ties and black suits and working as 'bouncers' in Belfast. Which pub or club could refuse such a 'service' — without suffering the consequences?

As for the UDA/UFF, they didn't have that level of business 'nous' or sophistication. The UFF bosses still on the streets turned to one quick, and big, earner: drugs. Not to use them, but to sell them. And who better, with time on their hands, and mobile phones in their hands, to organise and run a network of drugs supply and drugs dealers — than prisoners?

The rumours proliferated. Drugs-dealing gangs were set up and run throughout loyalist areas ... from behind bars.

At one stage, it was even reported by the *Sunday Times* that Johnny 'Mad Dog' Adair was having £1,500-a-week stashed into a secret bank account ... while he was still in prison.

The *Sunday World* carried many stories revealing what was going on, often from the mouths of prisoners inside using mobile phones to contact us.

The drugs culture had certainly taken hold outside the prison gates. 'Raves' were now rampant, where young people met to party. Ecstasy tablets and cannabis were avalanching into Northern Ireland in huge consignments.

By the time Adair got out of jail — and even, as the *Sunday Times* report suggested, while he was still in it — the UFF had taken a decision to exploit the illegal drugs business. It would do two things. It would help bolster the income of prisoners coming out of jail who still needed financial help. And it would line the pockets and make rich some of the men at the top: especially on Adair's 'home patch' of the lower Shankill in Belfast.

But it was a policy that was later to spark a bloody and brutal internal war: an internecine feud between Adair's UFF and the other major paramilitary bloc on the loyalist side, the Ulster Volunteer Force.

I recall one story that illustrates the paramilitaries' bare-faced contempt for public opinion. The *Sunday World* ran a story about kids of ten years of age and under, going to a block of derelict apartments at the bottom of the lower Shankill estate, the rundown and Kosovo-like housing project that was Adair's 'C' Company's base. The estate was like a UFF fortress, slogans daubed all over the walls, huge murals paying homage to the so-called 'Freedom Fighters', hard to get into, and even harder to get out of. The whole complex was built in a square shape, like an old military barracks.

And at the bottom were these derelict flats where drugs pushers were dealing in broad daylight.

But then we got a tip-off that kids as young as ten were taking taxis to buy E tabs from the dealers. Even taxi drivers who tippled to what was happening were sickened.

Our News Editor, Richard Young, did the story himself. We ran the story as the front page lead on a Sunday morning.

By Monday morning, new grafitti — other than the usual stuff eulogising the UFF — had appeared on the walls and doors of the flats. It mocked: 'ID [identification] REQUIRED — NO ONE UNDER-18 SUPPLIED'.

And there was the usual message to ourselves painted on the walls: 'F**K THE SUNDAY WORLD — OPEN FOR BUSINESS AS USUAL'.'

However, it wasn't only the *Sunday World* that was noting what was happening in UFF strongholds like the lower Shankill and in East Belfast. The UVF were watching, as well. And they didn't like what they were seeing. They didn't like Johnny Adair, either. And they really thought, in spite of what he had said in the interview at the start of this chapter, that he was a 'Mad Dog' who would eventually turn on them … as the next chapter explains.

14

Feud

'They're not the LVF. They're the DVF — for the Drugs Volunteer Force. And we want to expose them.'

The words of Bobby Jameson, a millionaire businessman from the tinderbox town of Portadown in County Armagh. He was on the streets of the town, painting over and pulling down wall murals and signs that supported the Loyalist Volunteer Force, who had split from the UVF years ago, and who Bobby Jameson was blaming, outright, for the murder of his brother, Richard. Richard Jameson himself was reported to be a UVF man, a commander in the mid-Ulster hotbed of sectarianism and strife. He had been involved in a huge Boxing Day bust-up with LVF men in the lounge bar of Portadown soccer club, which his family, and brother Bobby, had supported financially for a long time.

The poison between the UVF and the LVF had been sunk long before that, though, with Billy Wright's involvement in drugs.

The UVF didn't like that.

And UVF man Richard Jameson, according to sources close to his family, started building up a dossier on the County Armagh

LVF drugs dealers — at least three of them from the same family. Eventually, the LVF started to 'get heavy' with him. They visited his home. They threatened him. The hoods delivering the threat were captured on a security video camera at his home. Richard Jameson defied the LVF. He paid with his life. A car carrying two gunmen followed his jeep home one night. Close to his front door, they shot him dead.

The UVF were outraged. There was talk of a bloody feud in Portadown. Eventually, one Friday night in February 2000, two teenagers, Andrew Robb and David McIlwaine, were kidnapped after leaving a nightclub in the village of Tandragee, not far from Portadown in North Armagh. They were butchered with knives, their bodies abandoned on a lonely, winding country road to be discovered the next morning. They had multiple stab wounds. Their throats were cut.

One of the lads, David McIlwaine, was said to have been in the wrong place at the wrong time. The other, Andrew Robb, was accused of having been the driver of a 'scout' car used to stalk Richard Jameson before his murder. His mother, Anne Robb, has consistently denied this in interviews with the *Sunday World*. She has since raised the murder of her son with the NI Human Rights Commission based in Belfast. And she has supported calls for a special sub-Committee to be set up at Stormont in response to the spiralling drugs problem in the Province.

However, in spite of a gun attack targeting two loyalists with links to the LVF in January 2001, the UVF had not really started to 'avenge' the murder of Richard Jameson — until they shot dead Adrian Porter in March 2001 (see Chapter 19). And they still hate the LVF. They regard them as big-time drugs dealers: just like they see Johnny Adair's UFF 2nd Battalion 'C' Coy of the UFF based on the lower Shankill Road.

In the summer of 2000, with tensions still high between the UVF and the LVF, UFF man Johnny Adair started flirting with the County Armagh LVF and welcoming the presence of some of their leadership on the lower Shankill in Belfast. The portents of trouble with the UVF loomed large.

The whole combustible package busted wide open during a march on the Shankill in mid-summer. The date was a sun-splashed Saturday, 19 August 2000. Johnny Adair had organised a marching 'festival' on the road. Thousands of UFF/UDA men — and women — paraded up the Shankill and down the parallel Crumlin Road. Flute bands blattered out 'Kick the Pope' tunes on their flutes and drums. Crowds lined the pavements. Security forces reckoned there were 20,000 people in the parade and along the route.

But the parade was more than the innocuous 'festival' it was pre-billed as. It was intended as a full-scale 'show-of-strength' to warn the UVF to back off in the simmering tension of the loyalist estates of West Belfast. Adair played a card that infuriated the UVF, and exploded the volcanic feud between the UVF and the LVF which, over the next few days, would claim three lives — and spill over into another internecine loyalist vendetta in North Belfast, where four men would die at the point of blazing guns. He invited a contingent of Loyalist Volunteer Force members from Portadown and the town of Lurgan. And as if that wasn't enough to fly in the face of watching UVF men, a band sporting the LVF insignia on its base drum flew an LVF flag as well.

There was a knot of UVF men mustered outside the Rex Bar halfway up the Shankill Road. They were drinking outside, swallowing pints on the pavement in the bright sunshine — and getting more peeved by the minute at Adair and his entourage strutting along with their UFF and UDA banners. They had already dubbed his 2nd Battalion of the UFF/UDA's 'C' Coy on the Shankill Road the 'Ulster Dope Association', because of its reputation for drugs running.

Many of the UVF men gathered on the Shankill had been among the thousands of mourners at murdered Richard Jameson's funeral in Portadown. Many knew him personally. And the flaunting of the flag of the organisation that murdered him was the spark that lit the bonfire of the bitter, gun-toting feud that followed.

Said one eyewitness: 'It was simple. A UVF man stopped sipping a pint. He ran into the ranks of marchers and grabbed the LVF flag. All hell broke loose.'

A riot erupted. At least one gunman opened fire. Three people were wounded. Scores more were hit by flying fists, feet, bottles and bricks. Marchers were left with bloody heads, blood soaking down over their white shirts and tee-shirts. Heavily-armed troops and riot police were ordered into the area. But not before the UFF staged its most threatening show-of-strength yet. Adair and his East Belfast sidekick, multiple Milltown cemetery killer Michael Stone, had both been at the front of the parade. Neither were close to the gun incident. But they watched as guns came on to the streets. UFF guns. They were seriously deadly weapons. They were brandished by four masked men — and a black-clad balaclavaed woman in a short, hip-hugging mini-skirt.

Secretary of State Peter Mandelson pledged that video evidence would be used both to prosecute those involved in the riot, and in the gun-toting 'show-of-strength'. Very few were. And, at the time of writing, they cannot be identified for legal reasons. But guns had been brandished on the Shankill streets.

As the sun went down on that sultry summer Saturday night, terror chiefs on 'The Road' were already predicting that soon, there would be 'blood on the streets'. The prediction proved tragically true. Three men were to be gunned down in cold blood. And scores of families were to be hounded out of their homes on the Shankill, or face being burned out.

For the bullyboys, and girls, it was enough for a grandmother to have a grandson 'connected' with an organisation for her to be illegally evicted.

At one stage, the scale of the internal 'refugee' problem was massive. It was reckoned that 1,400 people — among them pensioners, women and children — had been left homeless in paramilitary purges. The crisis was so desperate that the housing authorities were even having to provide emergency shelter for those forced out of their homes — many at gunpoint — in the plush surroundings of the city's world-famous Europa Hotel. Something had to be done. And quick.

RUC Chief Constable Sir Ronnie Flanagan was in South Africa on a previously planned family holiday. A keen rugby supporter — he had played for the Ulster Provincial side as a hooker — he was hoping to see the Springbok tests against the touring Australians in Johannesburg and Durban. He saw them both on consecutive weekends. But only by sandwiching an emergency flight back to Belfast in between. The reason? To oversee the re-arrest of Johnny Adair and his dramatic return to jail. Stormont supremo Mr Mandelson, along with his security chiefs, had decided to revoke Adair's licence. Adair, thirty-seven, was first freed in September 1999, having served a third of his sixteen-year sentence for the self-confessed crime of directing terrorism. But, at the height of the Shankill feud the following August, Peter Mandelson issued the directive putting him back behind bars.

Anarchy was expected after Adair's arrest. Instead, it had the desired effect. The ordinary people of the Shankill had had enough. They were cowering in their homes at night not know-ing who was going to be targeted next, or who would be forced to flee by armed, masked men, or women. In one street of neat, red-brick houses alone — known on the Shankill as 'wee palaces' — *eleven* homes were lying empty and deserted, their contents strewn across front gardens and pavements. Poignantly, even a plastic Santa Claus, tucked away in a child's wardrobe for use the next Christmas, had been tossed out of an upstairs window, and was left lying on its head after looters had finished their work in the scarred street known as Shankill Terrace.

The Shankill internal loyalist feud settled down. But that wasn't the end of the loyalist internal vendetta. Go-betweens on both the UFF and UVF side set up behind-closed-doors attempts at reconciliation. They were, according to political spokesmen like Stormont Assemblyman David Ervine of the PUP, making headway. But the current of underlying tension between both paramilitary organisations was so strong it swept those negotia-tions away just weeks after gun law had ruled on the Shankill. And again, Adair was to be the focal — or, this time, vocal — point for violence to erupt.

This time, the feud hit North Belfast — another hotbed for loyalist paramilitaries of both hues, based along what came to be known as the 'Murder Mile', stretching from the UDA strong-hold of Tiger's Bay on the city's York Road to the UVF 3rd Battalion's base in the Mount Vernon flats (known to police anti-terror detectives as 'Mount Vermin'). Four men were to die — two from each side — at gunpoint over the seven days strad-dling what was dubbed the 'Halloween Horror' weekend of 31 October 2000.

It was Adair's name being bandied about in a gang fight that ignited the UFF vs. UVF feud in the North of the city. By this time, Adair had been locked up for more than two months, a dozen miles away from York Road, in Maghaberry jail, near Lisburn in County Antrim. But his profile among UFF men was still sky-high, especially among young, wannabe UFF 'freedom fighters'. Many of them had taken to wearing Celtic soccer jerseys, just like the shirts Adair had worn to stalk Catholic targets in nationalist areas. The difference was, the Celtic jerseys now had only one name on the back. And it wasn't the name of any of the team's star players. It was Johnny Adair's name printed on the green and white hoops on the soccer shirt.

I recall going to see a senior UDA man in the Tiger's Bay area as the feud peaked. I was anxious to know what had happened, how it had started, was it a roll-over from the August feud on the Shankill? But he told me the North Belfast bloodbath was ignited by taunts about Johnny Adair flying between two gangs of teenagers.

The UVF youth wing is known as the Young Citizens' Volunteers (YCV). The UDA/UFF youth wing has the title Ulster Young Militants (UYM). Between the YCV stronghold of Mount Vernon and the UYM hinterland of Tiger's Bay, on the York Road, is a big park: Alexandra Park. Gangs of teenagers go there at weekends, with carry-outs of beer or cider, to drink and play loud music under the cover of darkness.

On the night of Friday, 27 October 2000, two gangs were in the Alexandra Park. One was from the YCV faction in Tiger's Bay, the other was from the UYM in Mount Vernon. The senior UDA man told me a row erupted between the two gangs when insults were hurled by the YCV about Johnny Adair: about the allegations that he was a drugs 'Godfather', and that he injected steroids into himself to bulk up his body — both of which Adair has denied point-blank in interviews with myself and others. But when bodybuilders are taking steroids, they often inject the drug into themselves on the buttocks. Hence the jibe about some prisoners in jail 'having arses like pin cushions'. And hence one jibe in the park that sent the UFF young wannabes over the top: the YCV taunt that Johnny 'takes it up the bum'. That was the signal for a mini-riot to break out. The senior UDA man said that in the course of the scrap, one YCV boy from Mount Vernon was isolated and took a bad beating.

So the next night, Saturday 28 October, three carloads of UVF men from Mount Vernon — where 3 Company of the UVF is based — drove into the heart of the winding streets of Tiger's Bay. There were claims at the time, never stood up, that it was one of these UVF men's sons who had got the bad hiding the previous night. The convoy of armed UVF men cruised the Tiger's Bay streets. At the top end of the district, they spotted a group of young people on their way towards the top gates of Alexandra Park. They had plastic bags of carry-out beer and cider. It has not been established if they were part of the riot in the park the night before. The three-car convoy homed in on the walking group. A gunman in one of the cars leaned over the driver as the car pulled alongside the party-goers. The driver-side car window was down. Without warning, the gunman opened fire on the group. The driver, said to have been third in command of the UVF in Mount Vernon, is said to have almost hysterically screamed 'Kill them! Kill them!' as the cordite smoke from the gun stung his nostrils.

The assassin struck just one of his intended targets. He was David Greer, later acknowledged as a young UDA member. He fell fatally wounded at the top of Mountcollyer Street, dying in a pool of his own blood — just feet from the gate of the Alexandra Park where the jibes over Johnny Adair had started the row the previous night. And his murder signalled the start of the savage Halloween Horror loyalist feud in North Belfast.

Three more shooting victims were to die in the space of four days over Halloween. The timetable of death reads:

October 28. UDA volunteer David Greer gunned down.
October 31. The real Halloween Horror hits home. First, Bertie Rice, a former UVF Commander who had emigrated to South Africa but came home to work for the organisation's political wing, the Progressive Unionist Party, was murdered on his own doorstep. He was sixty-three, just two years off claiming the old age pension.

Then, as a huge fireworks display blasted off in the centre of Belfast, a former top UDA man, who was one of the Ulster Democratic Party's negotiating team at Stormont before the signing of the Good Friday Agreement, was slaughtered in front of his family in a tit-for-tat shooting. He was Tommy 'Inky' English, said to have 'retired' from the UDA three years previously because of ill-health, but who then became a UDP stalwart. Ironically, he was supposed to appear in court in Belfast the Thursday after his murder — on charges claiming he beat up customers in a city pub frequented by gays.

Finally, the fourth man to die was UVF man Mark Quail. It was another tit-for-tat feud killing. The twenty-six-year-old was shot dead in front of his girlfriend in a flat in the sprawling, mainly loyalist housing estate of Rathcoole on the Northern shore of Belfast Lough.

The gunmen who shot dead UDA man Tommy English had

pistol-whipped his wife as she tried to protect him. She walked behind her murdered husband's coffin at his funeral on the following Saturday 5 November — Guy Fawkes night. Doreen English had bruising on her face and a cut on her nose as, dressed in a dark pinstripe suit, and with a red poppy to remember the dead of two World Wars pinned to her lapel, she walked in the cortège with her three children. Up front, her husband's coffin was draped with the flag of the North Belfast battalion of the UDA. Flanking the coffin, and at times carrying it, were four masked men wearing berets, khaki military fatigues, and wearing black gloves and boots.

Also among the 2,500 mourners attending the funeral was a big contingent from Johnny Adair's 2nd battalion 'C' Company of the UFF on the lower Shankill. They amassed round the corner from the street where Tommy English's funeral was to take place from his mother's home in the heart of Tiger's Bay. Many of them were wearing black crombie overcoats — and they all had War Remembrance red poppies pinned to their coats, as had the masked men with their poppies pinned to their green berets. The Shankill 'team' marched up to the front of the house just as the funeral was about to leave. Adair's No. 2, a bulky individual in a black crombie, led them from the front, with 'Winky' Dodds at his side (Johnny Adair was still in jail). Their presence, coupled with the presence of the paramilitary-uniformed 'guard of honour', boded ill for the future of the feud.

Except for one important factor, picked up by the *Sunday World* for its front page story the next day. The headline running over the flag-draped coffin and the picture of the paramilitary-uniformed pall bearers read:

'TOP UVF MAN DEFIES DEATH — He turns up at UDA boss's feud funeral'.

That top UVF man was someone very close to Tommy 'Inky' English and his family. But his very presence at the funeral, unmolested and unharmed, meant that he had been given the OK to be there by UFF commanders. And, as the *Sunday World* revealed that day, peace talks had already begun to end the feud in Belfast — and put a stop to the Shankill feud, once and for all. All of that was accomplished in clandestine meetings between UFF/UDA and UVF negotiators.

Shortly after Christmas of the same year, it was announced that the joint leaderships had hammered out a peace pact and put in place an internal 'policing' arrangement whereby if trouble seemed to be boiling over again, so-called 'Provost Marshalls' would be called in to mediate. But that was too late for the seven men who had already died in the Shankill and North Belfast 'Murder Mile' feuds. And it was hammered out while Johnny Adair was still in jail.

At the time of writing, Adair is still behind bars — but fighting his case to get out. If he is kept in under the full terms of his sentence, and gets fifty per cent remission (he had served a third of his sentence when first released on licence), the earliest he can hope to be back on the streets is around the spring of May 2002. He did take his case to the Sentence Review Commissioners in Maghaberry jail. They first decided that he should be re-released. But then Secretary of State Peter Mandelson appealed that. He got a special hearing of the Commissioners in Maghaberry jail. And, just as he did when he flew back from South Africa in August to help put Adair back in jail, the RUC Chief Constable Sir Ronnie Flanagan backed up Mandelson in his bid to keep him there.

Adair was subsequently considering going for a judicial review in the Ulster High Court after the Commissioners overturned their original decision to free him having listened to Mandelson and Flanagan. But even though the Mandelson submission to the Commission was supposed to be 'in camera', inevitably details leaked out. And one of them — despite all his protestations to the contrary — links Adair directly to the growing drugs trade in Ulster.

The points that the Secretary of State underpinned to the panel of Sentence Review Commissioners were that:

- Adair had been involved in the procurement and distribution of guns and munitions.
- Adair had been involved in the 'authorisation of a number of paramilitary attempted murders and of a number of so-called punishment shootings'.
- Adair had orchestrated sectarian tensions and attacks in West and North Belfast and in Portadown in the summer of 2000.
- Adair had taken part in paramilitary shows of strength. (The *Sunday World* had run a picture of Johnny Adair in a hood at a UFF Press conference, and a picture of him without the hood, under a front page headline contrasting 'The Two Faces' of Adair. He never denied it was him in the hood.)

And then came the clincher on drugs:

- *Mr Mandelson alleged that Adair paid proscribed organisations from the proceeds of drugs dealing.*

That allegation, he assured the Commissioners, was made on the basis of top-level security force intelligence information. The

Commissioners obviously believed the Secretary of State, revoking their earlier decision to release Adair again. Explaining their decision later, they said they had received 'damaging information' during the two-day secret hearing in Maghaberry jail. Adair's advisors told him not to give his side of the story there. But the Review Commissioners concluded that they were 'persuaded' by the arguments put to them by Mandelson and Flanagan that 'the applicant (Adair) is likely, if released, to breach the terms of his licence.'

All a bit of a contrast with Adair's point-blank denial in interviews that he was *not* a drugs dealer or involved in the drugs trade. But then, there were question marks raised when, just months after his original release, he jetted off on a luxury holiday in the Bahamas. I asked him in an interview on his return where he got the money for that. He told me that was nobody's business but his own.

However, it subsequently became known that some of the top men in the UFF/UDA on the Shankill were using a secret bank account to 'launder' drugs money. CI6, the RUC's anti-racketeering squad, were investigating information that the bank account was in the name of a niece of one of the top men. And there were stories that, to counter the possibility that their assets would be seized if they were convicted of drugs pushing, the top ranks of the Shankill UFF/UDA had taken to buying expensive paintings. The claim was that they were paying cash for them. But they were telling the art dealers to put them into storage, or just leave them hanging in their galleries. In that event, if they were convicted and sent to jail — well, they could flog the paintings when they came out, have rolls of money in their pockets, and go back to what they were doing before they went in.

Said one senior police source: 'The money-laundering operations that drugs 'Godfathers' use are sophisticated. Some of these boys aren't as stupid as they look. Sometimes, they are as slick as the real Mafia 'Godfathers' in America. And sometimes, like in the paintings money-laundering scam, they pick up their ideas from that very source — the Mafia.'

Adair was reported to have a smile on his face behind bars on Wednesday, 24 January 2000. Because, while he was still considering a judicial review to try to get out of jail again, the man whose 'damaging information' had convinced the Sentence Review Commissioners to keep him there resigned as Secretary of State for Northern Ireland. Peter Mandelson fell on his own sword over the 'Domegate' passport scandal involving Indian businessman Srichand Hinduja. Ironically, at the time of the Mandelson resignation, sixty-three-year-old Hinduja was under investigation by the courts in India — over an alleged £6 million 'kickback' on an arms deal! Said one Maghaberry jail insider: 'Johnny had a wee self-satisfied smile to himself. After all, in one way or another, guns have played a very significant part in his life.'

15

The Florida Connection

'Lindy, you'd better have a look at this. I think we're going to have to go to work today ...'

We were on a family holiday in Florida — my wife, Lindy, News/Features Co-ordinator with the *Belfast Telegraph*, and our two boys. We were staying in one of our favourite places in America — Ireland's Inn (of all places!) on the beach in Fort Lauderdale. It's so-named because it's owned by a family called Ireland: we'd happened upon it by chance a couple of years back, got to know the people who own it and run it, and we go back whenever we're in Florida.

So we were there in August 1999. The weather was blistering hot. I jog. The only time to do that there is early morning. I was up, away, then in for a swim in the ocean. I went back to the hotel and bought a paper from a newspaper vending machine. When I lifted the *Miami Herald* from the machine, I could scarcely believe my eyes. Their front-page lead story was that an alleged and huge IRA gun-running operation had been uncovered in Fort Lauderdale. Three suspects, two of them from Belfast, another one from Cork originally, were to appear in a court in downtown Fort Lauderdale that day. It was to be the start of a Provo gun-smuggling epic that was to make headlines all around the world for over a year afterwards. It caused acute embarrassment to the Sinn Féin leadership back home: after all, the IRA were supposed to be on ceasefire. But it was also to prove that the IRA were intent on stocking up on new, 'clean' weapons, mostly handguns, which were to be used to purge more drugs 'Godfathers' back home in Ulster, and for use against allegedly 'anti-social' elements who the Provos either wanted to murder or maim in 'punishment shootings'. That was in keeping with the Provos playing the 'Protectors of the People' role by, in essence, setting up their own 'policing' force in the areas they dominate.

But the breaking news about the court appearances in downtown Fort Lauderdale was to lose both of us two days out of our holiday. On a story like that, holiday or no holiday, you go to work: it seemed too big to miss. And so it proved.

The alleged gun-running trio who appeared in the air-conditioned courtroom that day — the temperature outside was soaring towards the eighties — were Conor Claxton, then aged twenty-seven, Anthony Smyth (forty-two), and Siobhán Browne, formerly from Cork. Lindy filed stories back home to the *Telegraph* for the two days of the court appearance. I filed a two-page spread for the *World* for the weekend paper.

Another since-convicted gun-runner, Martin Mullan, then twenty-nine, was later picked up in Philadelphia. He too was brought back to the Fort Lauderdale court where the gun-runners, having been found guilty by a jury, were sentenced in late September 1999. But on that first day of the court appearances in Fort Lauderdale, there was much speculation among the Press posse that quickly gathered about which organisation back in Ireland the guns were bound for. It turned out they were being shipped back through the post, hidden in kids' toys and computer parts, among other things. Some seasoned hacks gathered there reckoned that was too 'primitive' a way for the Provo terrorist 'Godfathers' back home to operate. After all, they had already amassed an arsenal of guns and Semtex through secret large shipments, almost all in bulk and ferried by gun-running ships at sea, from Gaddafi in Libya, from the Soviets in the old days of the cold war, from the Balkans as war dissipated there, from sympathetic Palestinians in the Middle East, and, of course, from the USA itself. So the finger was being pointed at rebel republicans: dissidents like the Real or Continuity IRA, who had split from the Provos over the 'peace process' in the North after Sinn Féin members took their seats at the previously derided and hated Stormont, where, republicans claimed, unionists had misruled for seventy years.

But two men were adamant right from the start.

One was the US prosecutor Richard Scruggs, who spearheaded the gun-running case right from day one when the charges were laid, through to conviction and sentencing. And the other was FBI agent Mark Hastbacka, who had helped mastermind, along with the US's Alcohol, Tobacco and Firearms agency, the intricate and marathon surveillance operation that eventually snared the gun-runners.

Both of those hardened agents of the law pointed their index fingers at one organisation: the Provisional IRA.

And so it was to prove. By the end of the trial, it was reckoned — by the FBI, by Britain's secret service, and by the RUC Special Branch in Belfast — that the gun-runners had smuggled no less than 122 weapons into Ireland, some of them through postal addresses in Galway and beyond.

And there was controversy when the court case finished. The American jury acquitted the gun-runners of the most serious charges against them — smuggling arms to terrorists and conspiracy to maim or murder persons in a foreign country. That meant that the guru of the gun-running gang, Conor Claxton, got away with just a five-year sentence, the maximum for the charges he was convicted of under American law. The others involved got lesser sentences.

The verdicts left presiding judge Wilkie Ferguson furious. He hit the headlines in Britain, Ireland and Ulster when he fumed that Claxton's crime deserved the death penalty. The angry judge pointed out that under the guidelines governing Claxton's case, the Belfastman could only be sentenced to a maximum of five years and three months behind bars. Judge Wilkie blasted: 'If in a crack cocaine case a person can get a life sentence for possessing $400 worth of cocaine, this offence ought to have the death penalty.'

The analogy with drugs in the judge's hot-blooded statement was spine-chillingly, if subconsciously, ironic. Because that's why the Provos wanted the new, 'clean' guns for: dealing with drugs dealers. And they wanted to deal, again, in death. They wanted guns, handguns particularly, that had no previous 'form' — could not be traced to any previous IRA murders, and therefore could not endanger Sinn Féin's place at the political talks table, or, ultimately, at Stormont. They wanted guns that could fit into the 'no claim, no blame' killing closet. They wanted guns that could be used by the front organisation DAAD (Direct Action Against Drugs). And they wanted guns that could be used for specific killings, on however spurious grounds, and for so-called 'punishment shootings' — thus acting out their role as the 'people's police'. There was also a theory that if the IRA ever did decommission their existing arsenals — well, they would have a secret, new one, to fall back on.

As it has since turned out, major moves on decommissioning started in February 2000.

But before then, two men were to be shot dead with the new guns. One was a Belfastman, Charlie Bennett, the motive for whose death still remains a mystery. The Provos at first denied they carried out the killing of the Catholic man. But then, on a TV show I hosted with teenagers, most of them students, we were interviewing the Chief Constable of the RUC, Sir Ronnie Flanagan, a short time after the murder. He hadn't pointed the finger at any organisation up until then. The political 'peace process' in Ulster was on a knife-edge, with former Secretary of State Mo Mowlam walking a tightrope between success and failure. For Sir Ronnie to accuse the IRA of murder at that stage would have been political dynamite. But when one of the students asked Sir Ronnie, in the full glare of the TV cameras during the interview in his Knock HQ office, who he thought had shot dead Charlie Bennett, Sir Ronnie said he believed it was the IRA. So, the 'Godfathers' of terror had been pinpointed, again — and while they were on a 'ceasefire', too.

The news bulletins and the newspapers went to town. The theory was that it was one of the new guns from Florida, smuggled into Belfast, that was used for the Bennett murder. No one was ever convicted of the crime. Nor, at the time of writing, has the murder weapon been found.

Next in the sights of the IRA was a drugs 'Godfather'. Someone who also liked sunnier climes — not Florida, this time, but the Carribean. He was Edmund 'Big Edd' McCoy. But this time the DAAD killing would be different: for two reasons. The assassins would be using another 'clean' gun from the Florida consignment. And this time, there would be new DAAD killers on the block — fresh blood, still seasoned IRA men, but younger than the veterans who had started the drugs 'Godfathers' purge with the murder of Mickey Mooney in 1995. Instead, these would be IRA men with 'itchy fingers', proven terrorists who were backing the Gerry Adams/Martin McGuinness line in switching the republican strategy into politics, but still had the scent of cordite in their nostrils and the adrenalin-rush of close-quarter killing pulsing through their veins and senses.

McCoy was known on the streets of Belfast as a 'hard man'. He was a bare-knuckle prize fighter and he would take on anybody. He had been handpicked originally by Belfast's first 'Godfather', Mickey Mooney, when he was looking to build a team of 'minders' around him as he delved into the drugs dealing trade.

But just like Mooney, McCoy's fists, feet, or head were no match for flying bullets.

It was his prowess for throwing punches, in fact, that proved one of the reasons the Provos — aka DAAD — decided to take him out. 'Big Edd' McCoy had got into a 'digging match' with a top Provo — ironically, from what is known as the 'Bone' area of Ardoyne, an IRA stronghold in North Belfast. And, to use Belfast slang, McCoy 'gave him a digging'. He beat him, in other words. Badly. The Provos were unforgiving.

Two reports emerged of what happened after that. One suggested that the Provos had gone to McCoy and told him that he could literally pay for his life, rather than with it: if he immediately paid them a 'licence' fee of £10,000 to stay alive, *and* keep his drugs-running operation intact. Plus, he would have to keep paying the IRA their 'licence' fee on a regular basis. The other angle was that McCoy had made the offer to pay the £10,000 to the Provos — but that it was rejected.

Either way, McCoy was to pay the ultimate price, when DAAD cancelled his licence to live in the most brutal, and abrupt, manner imaginable. They shot him dead. As he sat drinking in a pub on a Sunday afternoon. Shades of Mickey Mooney, his original mentor, and 'Speedy' Fegan, with whom he once ran — both shot in bars, Fegan also on a Sunday afternoon.

In McCoy's case, he was in a suburban bar, in the sedate village of Dunmurry, on the South side of Belfast. The bar he was drinking in had been the scene of previous violence. It had been known as the Black Swan. The Provos had tried to bomb it during the Troubles. The punters drinking in it at the time were predominantly Protestant: the nearby Seymour Hill housing estate is a UDA/UFF stronghold. The patrons turned on the would-be bombers. They caught one of them. Only the police arriving from the nearby Dunmurry RUC station, just two hundred yards from the pub, saved his skin.

The pub had lain empty for a long time after that. But it had recently been taken over, renovated, and renamed. In keeping with Dunmurry's status as a 'village', it was re-christened the Motte and Bailey. It started attracting a more middle-class patronage, especially on Sundays.

McCoy knew he was in trouble with the Provos. He had 'disappeared' for a while. But, just like one of his former co-Godfathers, Brendan Campbell, he had come back to his old turf. One of his buddies told him he'd be safe enough that Sunday afternoon having a pint in peace in the Motte and Bailey. It was a set-up. When the DAAD assassins burst into the pub, McCoy didn't even hear the sharp crack of the gun before the bullets went into his brain, killing him instantly. Again, no claim, no blame.

After his death, McCoy's mother claimed he had been trying to 'go straight'. She even said she had given him the money she had been saving to buy a new car to try to help him start a new life. It wasn't to be. McCoy used the money to return to his old

ways. And, ultimately, to go the way of other drugs 'Godfathers'
— but this time, killed by the New Killers on the Block.

After the murder, a drugs contact of McCoy's got in touch
with me and provided photographs of McCoy living a life of
luxury while on holiday in the Caribbean. They show him
jet-skiing, womanising, wearing top-of-the-range designer
sportswear, sipping cocktails on the beach — displaying all the
hallmarks of the get-rich-quick young drugs dealer syndrome
that swept Ulster, and Ireland.

The contact told me that when Mickey Mooney was killed,
McCoy, who Mooney had first spotted as a protégé in jail, turned
to being a bouncer in the clubs and pubs of Belfast. 'Those were
the days when the bouncers were turning a blind eye, for a price,
to dealers operating inside the clubs. But then, the bouncers
started to realise that they could sell the drugs themselves — not
inside the clubs, but at the doors. So they did: asking clubbers,
many of them under age [under eighteen] on the way in: "Do you
want something to make you feel better?" They were selling the
E tabs for £5 each: cheap, when two bottles of beer inside would
cost you a lot, and you wouldn't get a similar buzz from the beer.

'But that started some "turf" wars between the existing
dealers and the bouncers like McCoy. And he could be brutal.
He felt he had to continually prove himself as a "hard man". I
remember once a man who had had a row with him was sitting
with his girlfriend in a pub. McCoy simply walked over to the
table, but instead of hitting the guy, he punched the girl right in
the face. Broke her teeth, broke her nose ... and then started on
her boyfriend.'

On another occasion, the contact said, McCoy had gone and
knocked at the front door of a rival with whom he was having a
row. When the man came to the door, the contact said, McCoy

immediately smashed him in the face, and beat him all the way up the hallway, putting his victim in hospital, after thrashing him to within an inch of his life.

McCoy was quick with his fists but he was also quick-witted. Once, when the police raided the home of Mickey Mooney's brother, drugs 'Godfather' Liam 'Fat Boy' Mooney, in Carryduff, just South of Belfast, there was £70,000 in the house, in banknotes — the proceeds of a drugs deal sealed earlier in the day. As the police broke down the front door with a US-style hand-held battering ram, McCoy grabbed the money, which was in two plastic shopping bags, dashed out the back door, legged it over the back garden wall, and sprinted away with the 'evidence'. He headed for nearby fields. There was a portacabin there used by workmen on a building site. He stuffed the £70,000 under the portacabin. And got away.

But he wasn't quick-thinking enough, or fast enough, to escape the Provos when they came looking for him in the Motte and Bailey pub.

But why, after fearing them and getting 'offside' for a while, did he come back? The drugs contact who supplied the pictures of McCoy in the Caribbean said: 'It was just like Brendan Campbell. He'd been shot once by the Provos. He'd gone away. He came back. Speedy Fegan had been shot. But instead of going away, he stayed. It's the scene they lock themselves into. The ready rolls of cash. The fast cars. The women attracted to both — and there are plenty of them. Their own crowd of cronies. The old cliche – "big fish, in a small pool". But I knew all of them. And at the end, it's almost a death wish. They seem to appreciate that they are going to die. But in the meantime, it's as if they are hellbent on living life to the full, before they do ...'

16

New Guns in Town

'The case on this bullet was the one we tried to shoot Adair with the first time. Tell him we won't miss him the next time. His name's on it.'

The note was cryptic, and to the point. It came into the office in a bubble-pack envelope. It was hand-written in capital letters. Inside, also, was a bullet. And it was meant as a warning, and a death threat, to UFF chief Johnny Adair.

A few weeks previously, he had been out on weekend parole from prison. It was shortly before he was to be let out on licence under the terms of the Good Friday Agreement (and before he was put back behind bars again because of the loyalist feud on the Shankill Road in the summer of 2000). Adair and his wife, Gina, who he'd married in prison — with a special cake baked behind bars, and sausage rolls and sandwiches made by other prisoners — had gone to a rock concert. The band playing was UB40, one of Adair's favourites. The venue was open-air: in the huge, green, railed paddock in the middle of Belfast's Botanic Gardens. The date was Friday, 30 April 1999.

There are those who say that Adair simply couldn't resist the temptation to see one of his favourite acts live on stage. There are those who say that Adair was there for another reason. He wanted his team, the UFF, to literally 'muscle in' on the lucrative security contracts for providing stewarding and bouncers at such mega-gigs, which were becoming even more popular in Belfast and other places as the Troubles subsided. And there are those who say that Adair was plain mad — as his nickname would suggest — for going anywhere near the concert in the first place.

The Botanic Gardens is nestled in the leafy suburbs of South Belfast. On one side of it is the architectural splendour of the buildings belonging to Queen's University. Along the perimeter runs the River Lagan. And not far away on the Eastern side of the Gardens lies the Lower Ormeau Road district, where both INLA and Provisional IRA cells were known to be bedded in throughout the Troubles.

Indeed, a prominent IRA man originally from the Lower Ormeau was known to be in the immediate precinct of the Botanic Gardens on the night of the rock concert. It was also known that he had been close to at least one of the weapons smuggled in from Florida by the Conor Claxton gun-smuggling clique. And he was very close to someone who was unpacking one of the guns in the Lower Ormeau district when the RUC's anti-terror Divisional Mobile Support Unit — known in the force as the 'Super Troopers' — swooped. So if there was one new, 'clean' Florida gun in that district ... well, it didn't take an Einstein to work out that there may have been others.

It wasn't hard to spot Adair. He was never one to hide his presence, or his persona, under a bushel. Like quite a few convicted terrorists, he thought of himself as a quasi-celebrity (they were seldom off the TV or out of the newspapers, after all). Everywhere they went in their own, tight-knit communities, they were fêted by people who hailed them as 'heroes', as Adair's later staged appearances at Drumcree with his cronies exemplified in the summer of 2000. So Adair's appearance at the Botanic Gardens rock concert, for whatever reason, was *not* low-key, or low-profile. And, perhaps incredibly, he didn't have too many of his 'minders' with him. He was lying sprawling on the close-cropped grass on the main, fenced-off, makeshift arena that warm Friday night with Gina — when he was almost shot dead!

There were many republicans who had sworn vengeance on Johnny Adair in return for the murder and mayhem he had masterminded as a self-confessed UFF 'director of terrorism'. Now, here was their chance. Adair had been spotted, inevitably. A 'runner' was despatched to get a gun: quickly. Within minutes, he was back. He used his 'pass-out' to get back into the concert arena. A gang of republicans approached Adair. A fight started.

'I felt a sharp pain in the back of my head, behind my ear,' Adair recalled. 'I was bleeding. I knew I'd been hit. I didn't know what with,' he said.

Somehow, he and his wife escaped. They got out of Botanic Gardens. Adair ended up in the Ulster Hospital at Dundonald in the early hours of the Saturday morning.

The next day, it was claimed that a 'sliver of metal' had been taken out of Adair's scalp. There were reports that it was the fragment of a hammer head or iron bar used to attack Adair.

To this day, Adair claims it was the splinter of a bullet that nearly killed him. Adair made the same claim to a hastily called news conference. His head was heavily bandaged, a huge white swathe sitting jauntily like a rugby forward's sweatband tilted sideways in the scrum.

' "MAD DOG" IS SHOT AT CONCERT' the *Sunday World* page 1 headline said, with the sub-head: 'Adair didn't know he had bullet in head'.

But did he? And had he? There certainly was scepticism. But then a contact on the republican side got in touch.

'Yes', he said, 'Adair was shot. They tried to assassinate him.'

So what had happened that, at such close range, the bullet had only struck Adair's head, leaving only a sliver of the lead behind his ear?

Two things, said the source. Either the bullet had been 'tampered with'. Or the ammunition was damp.

But who would have tampered with the bullet?

Either the American secret services, said the contact. Or the British MI6.

But how could they have got access to the gun?

'It was one of the weapons that came in from Florida,' said the contact.

So Johnny Adair could have been shot dead at the UB40 gig with a gun that was part of the Florida Connection.

As for us, we called in the police and handed over the bullet that had come into our office, the neatly written note that had come with it, and the envelope in which the latest Adair death threat — with its throwback to Florida — had arrived in. That's our public duty as a newspaper: no matter *who* is threatened — inform the police. The police are then under an obligation to tell the person threatened.

In any case, Adair found out about the threat, and the bullet. So did the UFF. And, as the *Sunday World* later revealed, the UFF put a death sentence on Florida gun-runner Conor Claxton. They have vowed that if he ever returns to Belfast, he is a dead man … just as so many republicans have vowed that, to them, Johnny Adair, for his 'past sins', is still a dead man walking — ceasefires or no ceasefires.

But, as they say in Belfast, there's more. It was a Saturday morning in the office. It was after Adair had been released on licence under the early terrorist prisoners release scheme. A phone call came in from a senior spokesman for the Ulster Democratic Party (UDP), the political wing of the UDA/UFF. On the line was John White, a convicted sectarian double killer who had served his time, and who had been part of the UDP talks team at Stormont in the red-hot negotiations running up to the signing of the Good Friday Agreement. Johnny Adair had got *another* bullet in the post that morning. But this time, it transpired, it was from his own side — loyalists, headcase militants who, in their accompanying note and threat, accused even Adair of being 'too soft on Fenians', and 'selling out'.

Would we come up, invited John White, meet Adair, and run the story next day? We're hacks. That's what we're paid to do. We went up to the prisoners' aid centre, which doubled as a UDP office, at the top of the Shankill Road. We were escorted into the converted portacabin-style extension at the back where Adair conducts his one-to-one interviews. Alwyn James, a photographer, was along, too. Adair arrived. He produced the death threat note. Then he produced the bullet sent with it. It was a huge bullet, like something that would be used in a high-powered rifle. Alwyn was taking pictures. Then, before I could tell him not to — police forensic detectives might later want to dust it for fingerprints — Alwyn lifted the bullet. He'd been in the army training corps at school. Innocently enough, he held the big bullet between forefinger and thumb. He began to say: 'I know something about these things ...' Whereupon Johnny Adair, dubbed 'Mad Dog' by the media, and a self-confessed 'Godfather' of terror, snatched the bullet from between Alwyn's fingers, and uttered the immortal words: 'From my experience, I think I know a wee bit more about these things than you ...'

Even in such circumstances — in the back of the main UFF HQ on the Shankill, in the presence of Adair, and with 'minders' on the door built like WWF wrestlers (and with, no doubt, a similar predilection for breaking bodies and bones) — we could hardly keep our faces straight. We bade our adieus, and left. Hurriedly. But when we got into our car parked in a side street round the corner from the UFF/UDP HQ, we couldn't help but have a bloody good laugh. 'Bloody' being the operative word ... given Johnny Adair's 'experience' at the concert. And, he was right: he did know a helluva lot more about bullets than either of us.

So there was mirth. And there was morbidity. Kate Kray, the ex-wife of the late Reggie Kray — one of the gangster Kray family from East London — wrote a book called 'Hard Bastards'. It was about the hardest men she's ever met. Johnny Adair was profiled. She later told me she was impressed by Adair. Said he was indeed one of top 'hard men' in Britain. And Adair was obviously impressed by Kate Kray. And by her late husband. For when Reggie Kray died — his horse-drawn hearse was pulled through the streets of East London as thousands thronged the pavement — Kate Kray revealed that among those of the 'hard bastards' portrayed in her book who sent condolences, one message came from Belfast. And who sent it? 'John Adair,' she replied, 'Johnny Adair.' A classic case, then, of one 'Godfather' paying his final respects to another.

17

Christopher 'Cricky' O'Kane — The Siege of Derry

'Up yours!'

The message from the one-fingered salute was unmistakable. The first finger, raised in the air defiantly as he strolled to court in sweatshirt and jeans, belonged to Derry's top drugs dealer, skinhead Christopher 'Cricky' O'Kane. The photograph appeared on the front of the *Sunday World* on 3 December 1999. The banner headline yelled: 'DRUG THUG'S GANG IS SMASHED'.

O'Kane was no stranger to the newspaper: or its front page. When the paper had previously named the top drugs dealers in Ulster under the front page headline of the 'SEVEN DEADLY SINNERS', he, along with the likes of 'Speedy' Fegan and Brendan Campbell — both later shot dead — was named among them. He didn't sue then. He hadn't, at the time of writing, sued since, even after a series of stories about him and his drugs-dealing gang.

Shortly after the 'Up yours' picture was snapped, the thirty-six-year-old drugs 'Godfather' ended up where he belongs — behind bars. He was jailed for ordering his henchmen to give a hiding to a bunch of teenagers. It was a brutal, baseball-wielding assault. 'Cricky' O'Kane and four of his henchmen pleaded guilty at Derry Crown Court to assault occasioning actual bodily harm. At the same court, three other members of the O'Kane gang pleaded guilty to possessing cannabis resin.

And while a smug and smiling O'Kane appeared defiant with the one-fingered salute, the folk he and his gang had terrorised in Derry were delighted. 'O'Kane was a ruthless, cruel, intimidating and terrifying thug,' said one resident of the Curryneirin estate where O'Kane had his base in Derry's Waterside district. But even though O'Kane was by then behind bars, the resident was still too afraid for his name to go into print.

Little wonder. The trappings of O'Kane's jet-setter lifestyle were apparent for all to see — even though he had the cheek to draw the dole every week. For someone allegedly not working, the Derry drugs baron drove a flash sports car (don't they all?), jetted out to sun-splashed holidays in Tenerife (where drugs are rife) and partied in posh restaurants (another trait of the get-rich-quick drugs 'Godfathers': Brendan Campbell was gunned down outside a trendy eaterie in Belfast).

His 'empire' stretched beyond the confines of Derry's ancient and famous walls. His minions ran drugs into towns like Limavady in the East of the Province, the British army garrison town of Ballykelly, through into the university town of Coleraine, with its hefty student population, and into the town of Dungiven, at the foot of the Glenshane Pass linking the main road from Belfast to Derry and Donegal. Once out of jail, he ran a string of minions, or small-time dope dealers, called mules, into the tourist resorts of Donegal, like the seaside towns of Bundoran and Buncrana.

But, again, his drugs-running operation was not without risk. The skinhead who ran his gang with an iron fist was lucky to escape a lead bullet — as with so many drugs dealers — from the IRA. That was in 1995, when a posse of armed Provos burst into a house where they believed he was staying. The masked men rampaged into a bedroom, hoping to find O'Kane asleep. But they'd picked the wrong place.

That was six years ago, which shows how long O'Kane has been running his mini drugs empire, and his campaign of terror against anyone who got in his way, including local residents of the Curryneirin estate where he lived and which he used as his criminal base.

Police sources say that O'Kane was once a member of the ruthless republican terror group, the Irish National Liberation Army. However, the same sources say he fell foul of the organisation after an Armalite rifle went missing. The gun was later used to hold up a post office when £15,000 in hard cash was stolen. They say that helped O'Kane set up his drugs-running underworld in Derry.

As for the rest of Derry City and its surrounding County, the drugs scene is dominated by smaller dealers. The Provos, while 'licencing' some dealers, are like their counterparts in South Armagh. They believe that being involved directly with drugs is seen as 'dirty business' — especially among Sinn Féin voters. That's why in places like South Armagh, and Derry (both places close to the border) the IRA is more into the smuggling of livestock, diesel, cigarettes and booze.

The livestock smuggling backfired, badly, in February of 2001 — with an outbreak of the dreaded foot-and-mouth disease in South Armagh. The focus swung powerfully on to cross-border smugglers then. The Stormont First Minister, David Trimble, who is also leader of the Ulster Unionist Party, pulled no punches when he pointed the finger, blaming the outbreak of the plague on the 'culture of South Armagh where people think they can do whatever the Hell they like'.

And there were plenty of people in the Republic of Ireland, where the economy is anchored by the agricultural industry, who suddenly jettisoned their notions of smugglers, no matter who was masterminding them, being some kind of romanticised felons: jack-the-lads just bucking the system, like poteen makers. Ireland's legions of farmers, in particular, envisaged their livelihoods literally going up in smoke as burning barricades of infected sheeps' carcasses flared along the South Armagh skyline. Said one farming broadcaster in Belfast: 'In large parts of rural Ireland, the so-called romance of the smuggler went up in those animal carcass pyres as well.'

But as for drugs in Derry, outside of the likes of the main 'Godfather', 'Cricky' O'Kane, the attitude towards dealers was perhaps encapsulated by what happened to one of the city's former most prominent Sinn Féin activists. He is Hugh Brady. He was caught carrying cannabis while going on a fishing trip. And when Sinn Féin found out — whether it was merely for public relations reasons or not — he was dropped ... hook, line and sinker, as they say.

Recently, another much-respected Derry politician has entered the war against drugs. He is the joint-Nobel Peace Prize winner, Euro-MP, MP and, until recently, Stormont Assembly member, John Hume. He reckons that Derry has not seen the development of major drugs ghettos like those on the UFF-controlled Lower Shankill Road in Belfast. But during the loyalist feuds in Belfast in the summer and autumn of 2000, and when loyalist paramilitaries started pipe-bombing Catholic homes again, he warned of such terrorist campaigns being waged for ulterior motives — as a cover-up, essentially, for a criminal core at the heart of such organisations as the UFF in West Belfast, to camouflage their wider drugs-running operations.

Ex-INLA man 'Cricky' O'Kane, meanwhile, was out of jail and back at what the Provos in Derry call the 'dirty business' of drugs dealing.

And at the time of writing this chapter, another *Sunday World* reporter has had to make a report to the police about some information emanating from Derry.

He was advised to look under his car every morning before going to work.

The Sequel

But then there was, 'Jesus, they've almost cut him in half!'

Those were the words of one of the first eyewitnesses to rush to the scene of the shooting in Derry's Curryneirin estate. The gunmen were from the IRA.

The victim? Cricky O'Kane.

The weapon used? Unusually for the Provos, a sawn-off shotgun.

O'Kane, thirty-seven, was single. He lived alone in Milldale Crescent, in the Curryneirin estate, where he had terrorised local residents for years. But in the early hours of Saturday 21 April, he left that modest house — albeit ringed by security cameras, and with a new anti-intruder system installed just weeks previously — to go out on 'business', as drugs dealers do.

He thought he knew how to take care of himself. After all, the ex-INLA man had survived three previous attempts on his life, once thanks to his newly installed security measures. That kept a previous IRA killer gang at bay.

This time, however, a four-man Provo 'hit squad' was waiting *outside* his home. As he walked across waste ground to get to one of his flash cars, they struck. The gunman wielding the 'clean' sawn-off shotgun went straight for O'Kane: he blasted him in the stomach — up to six times — with buckshot. Such a fusillade at such close range almost cut O'Kane in half, as one of the first eyewitnesses who rushed to the murder scene so graphically observed.

And thus, another of the drugs dealers named by the *Sunday World* as 'Ulster's Seven Deadly Sinners' was dead.

Ironically, it came at a time when he'd just pulled off the biggest drugs coup of his life. That started with a huge cache of heroin, cannabis and E tabs being shipped undercover into Cork harbour.

O'Kane was doubling up for the first time with a gangster family from North Dublin. The drugs were smuggled North via Limerick, Sligo, Letterkenny, and then across the border into Derry. At one stage, one of his cronies transported some of the drugs with a woman accomplice, under the cover of a blanket in a pram, with a baby in the pram!

Ironically, when O'Kane's runners picked up the huge consignment in Limerick, they paid only half what was owed as a down payment. O'Kane was to pay off the other half of 'the cut' when the drugs were sold. Instead, just three weeks after the huge haul was smuggled across the border, it was he who was almost cut in half.

18

A Voice from the Grave

"Cueball" remembers you — from the grave ...'

The pencil-slim, six-foot punter in the knee-length overcoat was shaking my hand as he said it. The handshake wasn't friendly. He looked me straight in the eye. His eyes were cold, and threatening.

I was at the Ulster Amateur Boxing Senior Finals in the Ulster Hall in Belfast. Earlier, I'd gone to the toilet during a break in the bouts. But two 'heavies' followed me in. One started giving me stick about a piece I'd written in the paper after INLA chief Hugh 'Cueball' Torney's murder (see Chapter 4), about him threatening to shoot a reporter dead.

I walked out of the toilet. It's not good arguing in those circumstances. The gents' was bunged with other boxing fans. Other people around, although unaware of what is going on, often offer the greatest protection in that they are potential witnesses to an attack. Not that that often deterred the INLA. However, I went out and took my seat. I had a couple of young boxing fans with me. I was more worried about them than I was about myself. Anyway, I had a few mates sitting a couple of rows behind me in the stalls.

But even before I could tip them off to what had happened in the lavatory, the third guy — the one in the knee-length overcoat — approached my seat. He leaned over a couple of rows that were in front of me. He held out his hand. Innocently, I took it. As he shook it, he looked me in the eyes and said, coldly: 'Cueball remembers you — from the grave ...'

I felt like punching him. But I had the two young fans with me, sitting beside me. I didn't know what he had up the overcoat, what he may have been carrying. He turned on his heel, and walked off into the boxing crowd. I waited a few minutes. I alerted my friends in the seats up behind us. Later, they escorted me to my car. There were a few boys who could handle themselves among them, boxing aficionados from way back. But fists seldom count when faced with firearms. Something could have happened to me. But if it was going to, I didn't want it happening in front of the youngsters with me. I will be forever grateful to those lads: I'm not naming them here, but they know who I'm talking about.

Nothing came of that incident. But the shadow of INLA gunman Hugh 'Cueball' Torney still ran its writ — even from the grave. And that was to manifest itself in a savage murdering and mutilation match in a deserted factory in early October 1999. The tentacles of Torney's terror gang had infiltrated the Dublin drugs scene long before his death. Two of his INLA successors in Dublin were Belfastmen Declan Duffy and Pat Campbell.

Duffy, in his mid-thirties was, at the time of writing, in jail in the Republic. Pat Campbell, then aged twenty-two, is in his grave, having been hacked to death in the factory faction fight in which at least seven other men were seriously injured, and which came to be known as the 'Ballymount Bloodbath', after the bleak industrial estate where the factory was sited.

The *Sunday World's* Chief Crime Reporter in Dublin, Award-winning Paul Williams — he also wrote the book *The General*, based on the gangster life, times and death of Martin Cahill, subsequently made into a film of the same name — explained how Duffy and his INLA gang had tried to muscle in on Brian O'Keefe's drugs fiefdom in Dublin.

He dubbed what happened in the empty factory 'the most savage and gruesome confrontation in Irish gangland history'.

Paul wrote: 'On one side was a loose collection of criminals led by Brian O'Keefe — a [then] twenty-nine-year-old drugs dealer from Walkinstown in West Dublin ... on the other [was] Belfast-born terrorist Declan Patrick Duffy, a bully-boy thug who uses the IRA as a front for criminal racketeering.'

O'Keefe himself was getting rich grabbing slices of the break-up of another drugs 'Godfather's' multi-million empire after the murder of campaigning journalist Veronica Guerin. And four years previously he had been suspected of ordering a gun attack on one of Martin 'The General' Cahill's top 'minders', a hardman known as 'The Viper'. Now, however, he was entering the big league himself — with up to thirty thugs aligned to his operation.

A summary of Paul Williams's story reveals that Declan Duffy had once boasted to a *Sunday World* reporter that he had shot people in the past and was second-in-command of the INLA in Dublin. One of his cronies — John Morris, twenty-seven, from Tallaght in West Dublin — was shot dead by the Garda Síochána in June 1997 after an armed robbery. By late 1999, however, Duffy wanted part of bearded O'Keefe's burgeoning drugs business.

At one stage, the INLA kidnapped O'Keefe himself. He was allegedly taken to a flat in North Dublin and tortured. He claimed he escaped. But associates of his later claimed he'd paid what amounted to a 'licence fee' of up to £58,000 to the INLA to keep operating. And, they said, he spilled the beans — confidentially, he thought — and revealed he'd also handed over a cache of sixteen weapons to the INLA as part of the deal.

But it wasn't to end there. One of O'Keefe's cohorts was later attacked by a friend of one of Duffy's INLA men. According to Paul Williams, a team from O'Keefe's mob went looking for the attacker the following night. They smashed their way into a house. Their quarry fled up into the attic. But the revenge squad couldn't get him down — even though they rammed a sword up through the ceiling to try to stab him!

A rendezvous was arranged between both gangs, purportedly to hammer out a peace pact, known in Dublin gangland slang as a 'straightener'. Part of the 'peace package', it later turned out, was payment of compensation for damage to a van. The venue was the deserted factory in the bleak Ballymount industrial estate. The date was the night of 6 October 1999. Paul Williams's account of what happened reads:

'The tension was beginning to build. On the night of the bloodbath O'Keefe sent six of his cronies up to the industrial estate. He remained outside while they walked into a nightmare. They were surrounded by Duffy, Campbell and three other INLA men. The INLA men were carrying guns. They tied up O'Keefe's duped 'intermediaries' at gunpoint. And then they started to torture them.

When he heard their screams for mercy outside, O'Keefe went back to his house in Walkinstown and summoned help. He and eleven others sped up to the factory in a van and gave the INLA a severe beating. Duffy and his cohorts were in the process of dumping O'Keefe's battered and bloodied pals into a van. They had just dismantled their guns and had put them in a hold-all bag in the middle of the factory floor.'

In the course of the O'Keefe gang's 'rescue', Duffy's co-Belfast cohort, Pat Campbell, was hacked to death with hatchets and knives. He was later buried in a paramilitary-style funeral in his native West Belfast. Duffy himself was lucky to escape with his life, as were his 'comrades-in-arms' caught with him. They suffered serious wounds. As did O'Keefe's bruised, bloodied and broken-limbed crew. One man had both his legs broken during the INLA 'torture' session.

At the end of his October '99 report of the bloodbath, Paul Williams wrote: '... one thing is certain: the feud between Duffy and O'Keefe is far from over.'

How right he was. Late on the night of Friday, 26 January 2001, a nightclub bouncer in Dublin narrowly escaped death when a booby-trap bomb exploded under his car. The bomber's target, Declan Draper, twenty-two, was reportedly a friend of the six men ambushed in the Ballymount factory by the INLA. His family said he was not a criminal. But Irish army bomb experts said the bomb bore all the hallmarks of an INLA booby-trap device. On this occasion, it misfired — directing the blast downwards, rather than up under the driver's seat.

Drugs Squad detectives believed, however, that no matter who the bomb was meant for, the motive was revenge — for the 'Ballymount Bloodbath' that claimed the life of Belfast INLA man Patrick Campbell eighteen months earlier. Said one senior Dublin detective investigating the bomb murder bid: 'This was a revenge attack and a very disturbing escalation in this feud.' The bomb attack came two weeks after Declan Duffy and another INLA man, Paddy O'Toole, were jailed for nine and seven years respectively.

The Dublin bomb incident occurred just twelve hours after bomb squad officers in Limerick had defused another gangland device. Paul Williams wrote: 'The bomb, it is believed, was to be used in an attack in the ongoing feud in the city, which has already claimed the life of Eddie Ryan. Ryan, forty-one, was gunned down as he drank in a (Limerick) city pub last November (2000).'

'Since then there have been several gun attacks in the city and Gardaí have been struggling to prevent an all-out bloodbath between two gangs which number over forty hardened criminals.'

A Garda source was quoted as saying the two gangs were 'extremely well armed'. And Garda Commissioner Pat Byrne was clearly concerned about both bomb incidents, especially the INLA 'revenge' bomb in Dublin. He said at the time: 'This is a very serious development. This is an aspect of criminal behaviour that we haven't had to contend with before. We are not prepared to allow this kind of situation to escalate.'

But, as far as Dublin was concerned, anyway, the ghost of ruthless IRA gunman Hugh 'Cueball' Torney was still haunting that city from the grave … as the stories focusing on both 'graduates' from his 'university of terror' in Belfast, Declan Duffy and the murdered Patrick Campbell, proved.

19

Current Affairs

'I do not do drugs. I do not deal in drugs. I want none of my nine children, or any of my grandchildren, to become involved in drugs.

'I was not on drugs, contrary to rumour, when I did what I did at Milltown cemetery. I did that because I was at war, and the people who died were casualties of war. They were not my intended targets. To this day, I maintain that my targets on that day were Gerry Adams and Martin McGuinness ...'

The words are those of Michael Stone, the loyalist multiple assassin who murdered, among others, three people at the funeral of the IRA's Gibraltar Three, Mairéad Farrell, Sean Savage, and Danny McCann, on 16 March, the day before St Patrick's Day 1988. It was an act that almost sparked civil war in Ulster, a war which could have spread South of the border, too.

Just three days later, at the funeral for one of Stone's victims — IRA volunteer Caoimhin MacBradaigh, a thirty-year-old taxi driver — two British army corporals drove alongside, and then, reversing in panic, into the cortège. In plain clothes, Corporals Derek Wood, twenty-four, and David Howes, twenty-three, both from the Royal Signals Regiment, were dragged from their car and disarmed when they drew their guns — Cpl Wood had fired a shot in the air from his Browning pistol. They were beaten and stripped to their underpants and then they were carried and kicked into the GAA stadium at Casement Park in Andersonstown, West Belfast. From there, they were driven in a black taxi 220 yards to waste ground and shot dead — one of them shot six times, the other five — as they lay, unconscious, on the ground. It was a brutal double murder that stunned the world when TV pictures were flashed round the globe.

It was a similar story with the Milltown massacre. Along with IRA man MacBradaigh, two civilians, Thomas McErlean, twenty-two, married with two young kids, and John Murray, a twenty-six-year-old father-of-two, died in the cemetery onslaught. Stone had been badly beaten, too, when a crowd of chasing mourners at the Milltown cemetery massacre caught up with him on the hard shoulder of the M1 Motorway, which flanks the cemetery, at the start of the main Belfast–Dublin road route. Armed riot police in Land Rovers rescued him. But not before his pursuers had stolen one of the handguns he used on that infamous day.

He was later sentenced to a string of life sentences for the Milltown triple murder, and three other assassinations he later confessed to, which, he said, he carried out as a loyalist 'soldier' linked to the then Ulster Defence Association, later to become known and carry out its killing operations as the Ulster Freedom Fighters. In all, Stone was convicted of six murders — the other three were Sinn Féin member Patrick Brady in 1984, and Catholic workers Kevin McPolin (in 1985), and Dermot Hackett in May 1987. When he eventually appeared in court, he was also charged with six attempted murders and thirty-two other terrorist-related charges.

However, like many other terrorist prisoners — both loyalist and republican — he was released from the Maze jail (since closed) in the summer of 2000 under the terms of the Good Friday Agreement. At the Press conference that Stone staged on the day of his release, I asked him if the thirty-one-year terrorist war that had ravaged both Ireland, and Britain — and sometimes the European Continent with the murder of British soldiers and the bombing of British military bases — was finally over. In front of a battery of reporters and TV cameras, his reply was: 'For me, personally, the war is over.' The Press conference was staged in East Belfast. Stone is from East Belfast. While in jail, he was the Commanding Officer of the UDA/UFF prisoners in the Maze.

Since getting out of jail, he has travelled to Glasgow to support his favourite football team, Glasgow Rangers FC. While over there for one of their matches — an 'Old Firm' game against arch-rivals Glasgow Celtic — he posed for pictures in the Scottish city's plush Hilton Hotel. Word got out about Stone staying there. The hotel was targeted for a hoax bomb call deep into the sleet-ridden night before the match, and had to be evacuated, with many people going out on to the wind-swept, freezing streets in their pyjamas. Stone dandered down from the floor he was staying on — the lifts are out of bounds in such an emergency: emergency stairs and exits have to be used instead — and even carried the bags of a Belfast businessman he met en route. The businessman was a Catholic, and a Celtic supporter to boot. Stone didn't appear to either know, or mind. He deposited the man's bags in the lobby. What a change from killing Catholics to humping their bags for them, especially in a hotel where a bomb scare had been sparked by his very presence!

However, being that close to one (respected and law-abiding) Celtic supporter was enough. Stone decided the next day not to go to the game, watching it instead on TV. He said he believed his presence could provoke trouble between the rival, highly charged-up fans. We in *Sunday World* got the pictures of Stone and his fellow 'fans' from East Belfast posing with Rangers players Tore Andre Flo, recently signed from Chelsea, and the Dutch international Ronald de Boer. We splashed the Stone picture on the front page. Rangers — and a lot of other people — were not amused.

Accompanying Stone in Glasgow that weekend were a number of senior UFF figures from East Belfast. As with the lower Shankill on the other side of the city, drugs dealing is rife in UFF-controlled areas. As an ex-UFF Commander himself, a finger of suspicion pointed — without any basis in fact — at Stone himself. So the question had to be put: was Michael Stone involved in any way in the drugs trade?

Richard Sullivan, the News Editor, and myself met him on 16 March 2001. It was the thirteenth anniversary of the Milltown massacre. I had met Stone at a function the previous night, and he said he wanted to talk. The main core of that conversation and interview was about him regretting that he had caused pain to other people and their families when his main targets at Milltown, he still insisted, were the Sinn Féin leaders Gerry Adams and Martin McGuinness, both of whom were at the graveside when Stone's shrapnel grenades, and bullets from two guns, (a Browning 9mm pistol and a Ruger .357 revolver), started to fly.

But Stone also talked about other things: like the possibility of loyalist paramilitaries breaking their 1994 official ceasefires ('official', because, unofficially, they have killed people since: not least during the internecine feud of summer 2000) because of the Real IRA's bombing campaign. Just days before, RIRA had planted a 'spectacular' in the heart of London, blasting the BBC's TV Centre in Wood Lane, purportedly in 'revenge' for a Panorama programme about the bombing of Omagh.

And Stone revealed, for the first time, that he was not altogether a 'loner' when he murdered at Milltown cemetery. He said that two UDA 'Brigadiers' knew about his one-man assassin spree bid. He refused to name them when we asked.

However, having shot at least one man — Thomas McErlean, who, even to this day, he describes as 'brave: he was unarmed, facing my guns, don't forget' — at almost point-blank range at Milltown, Stone denied point-blank that he was using, or dealing in, drugs. Stoney-eyed, he looked straight into mine and without blinking, without flinching, made the quotes carried at the top of this chapter. 'I do not do drugs. I do not deal in drugs.' And when I named a bar to the North of Belfast where, it was alleged, he had been spotted dealing drugs, he said: 'I was there to meet a man about a dog.' And, poker-faced, he claimed that he keeps no less than seven dogs — five of them, he said, for 'security' reasons.

Michael Stone was sitting in his painting studio, burrowed away deep in his native East Belfast. He has since moved because, he said, he was being stalked by the Real IRA. You had to travel through a labyrinth of winding streets to get to it. And we followed him in a car being driven for him by another man — just like the dogs, for 'security' reasons. And when he insists he is not on drugs, or dealing in them, he also states that none of his nine children — he has been married twice, and was contemplating a third wedding in July 2001 if, as he quipped, 'Drumcree doesn't get in the way' — are into drugs either. He says that he wants it to stay that way. He also says, with a noticeable degree of paternal pride, that none of his offspring have become involved with paramilitaries, adding that he wants that to stay the same way, too.

But not far from where Stone sits carefully dabbing the finishing touches to an exotic, if not erotic, painting of a mermaid, specially commissioned by a Belfast businessman, sits the glaring and indisputable evidence of more paramilitary activity. A charred, derelict and ransacked house — and its outbuildings — is close by to where we are talking to Michael Stone. Until recently, a drugs dealer called Adrian Porter lived in the house. He had connections to the Loyalist Volunteer Force drugs runners in Portadown, County Armagh. It was the LVF who shot dead Portadown businessman Richard Jameson outside his home, which sparked the loyalist feud that was later to rage on Belfast's Shankill and Shore Roads.

Richard Jameson, an alleged UVF commander, had started compiling a dossier on LVF drugs running. After his death, his brothers started a propaganda blitz against the LVF, labelling them the DVF — for Drugs Volunteer Force — though they appealed for no tit-for-tat retaliation. The UVF thought otherwise. And they blamed Adrian Porter (who was, like Johnny Adair and leading LVF members, a muscle-bound bodybuilding enthusiast — tapes of bodybuilding contests were found in his charred former home) for supplying the getaway car used in the murder of Richard Jameson.

They swore revenge. The house Adrian Porter lived in on the corner of where two roads split into a 'Y' junction as they run out of Dundonald in East Belfast was first torched. Outhouses were gutted, too. And the walls were daubed with messages linking the LVF to drugs. But it wasn't just the Jameson murder that Porter, after his death, was linked to. The torched house he had lived in was just over a mile from a bird sanctuary duck pond where a Scottish loyalist had been brutally murdered. Police sources say he had fallen foul of Porter and another Ulster loyalist with heavy links into terror gangs. Porter and the other Ulster loyalist lured the Scot to the lonely duck pond. Porter hit him over the back of the head with a hatchet. The other boy finished him off with a bullet to the head. At the time, a fallout over drugs money was suspected to be behind the crime. And Porter, according to loyalist sources, was up to his neck in drugs dealing at the time of his death.

However, the burning of the dwelling he lived in was the first warning that UVF gunmen intended taking retribution for the Jameson death and 'other matters'. He went on the run for his life. He told friends he knew gunmen were looking for him. And on the night of Tuesday, 13 March 2001, they caught up with him. He was in a house in the sleepy village of Conlig, best known for being the place that spawned Grand Prix racing driver Eddie Irvine, and not much else. Next morning, Conlig was to hit the headlines. On that Tuesday night bullets were sprayed through the window of the house where Porter was talking in the living room with another man. Porter went down fatally wounded. The other shooting victim was hit, but survived. And the word was that the Porter killing was the work of the UVF, still exacting retribution for the murder of Richard Jameson.

But that wasn't the only drugs-related murder to pockmark the opening months of 2001. Just a week into the New Year, on Saturday 6 January, Hugh Jordan and I had finished work early in the afternoon. The paper looked to be wrapped up, with a good front-page lead story after the holiday week. We nipped across town to the Cregagh Road to Gibson Park, the home of Malone Rugby Football Club. We're both members (unfortunately now, because of our ages, 'non-playing') of what are known locally as the 'Creggie Road Red Sox'. We were there to enjoy a good match: Malone were winning, and had just scored a spectacular try. And we had hoped to enjoy a good pint, too. But just minutes after arriving, a police contact we know dandered over and said: 'You boys would be as well getting yourselves up to the Clontonakilly Road on top of the Castlereagh Hills. There's a body lying up there.'

The road we were tipped off about was only a few minutes drive away, overlooking East Belfast. Two of the main drugs dealers we knew lived in big houses in that area. We thought it could be one of them. When we got there, the police at the scene were puzzled. They couldn't identify the murder victim. One of the officers had pictures of the murder scene on a digital camera, with the victim's bruised and bloodied body clearly visible. But the face was bloated, as if he had taken a severe hammering before being killed. We were asked to stay behind a few minutes after the rest of the Press pack left. We were shown the images on the digital camera, purely to see if we could help the police on the ID front. As usual, it was a sickening sight. However, we had to tell the police it wasn't any of the local dealers we knew.

Within minutes of leaving the scene, however, we were contacted by a political source. Word was already out. The murder victim was said to be Geordie Legge, a former UDA Commander in East Belfast. From Island Street, in the shadow of David and Goliath, the giant Belfast shipyard cranes, Legge was linked to the murder of another UDA Commander, Ned McCreery, way back on 14 April 1992. Now, it seemed, that murder had come back to haunt him — to his death. He had already been stabbed by a close acquaintance of McCreery, but had survived that murder bid. He had been linked to the murder, by stabbing, of a man at a soccer supporters' club, also in East Belfast, as well as the murder of a security guard. Now, it was also being alleged that he had 'done in' — stolen for his own use — £30,000 of UFF drugs-trade money.

Word on the street was that on the evening of Friday 5 January, he was 'invited' by a phone call to his home to a bar for a 'meeting'. He went through the front door of the bar walking. Murder squad detectives believe he was carried out later that night, under cover of darkness, his stabbed, battered and mutilated body wrapped in a blood-soaked carpet. They have never been able to find the bar lounge carpet: in spite of raiding another pub where they thought the carpet may have been taken and burned in a metal wheelie bin after the dumping of Legge's corpse. And the murder hunt detectives had not, until the time of writing, found Legge's killers, either.

He had died such a tortuous and obviously brutal death that his face was bloated and blackened, his T-shirt was shredded by the multiple stab wounds that killed him, and the denims and trainers he was wearing were red-soaked by blood. In the old days, the UDA used to murder people like that in what were called their 'Romper Rooms' in clubs or shebeens, sometimes dropping breeze-blocks on their heads as the horrific coup-de-grace. This time, with the Legge murder, it looked like the 'Romper Room' syndrome had come back from the grave. And in a final, Mafia-like touch — perhaps alluding to the claim that Legge had 'done in' drugs money — Geordie Legge's body was dumped on the isolated Clontonakilly Road high in the Castlereagh hills ... with the pockets stuffed full of fake banknotes.

And therein lay yet another link to two other brutal, Mafia mob-style, and drugs-linked murders. The first occurred just three weeks before Legge's murder, at the start of Christmas week 2000. It was Monday 19 December, when the body of William James Rockett was discovered on waste ground. Again, just like

Geordie Legge, he was linked to drugs dealing. Again, just like Legge, he was reported to have committed a 'crime' against a local UDA Commander: this time in North Belfast, not the East of the city. Allegedly, and unlike Legge, he wasn't directly involved in the murder of a UDA Commander: instead, he had tried to torch his house after a row. And, again, just like Legge, when his body was discovered, the pockets of his trousers were stuffed with paper money. Another Mafia-like signal that Rockett was involved in drugs.

And so it subsequently proved. He had gone on the run after trying to petrol bomb the former UDA Commander's home. He sought sanctuary in the ranks of the drugs-dealing LVF in Portadown. But when the UFF — who had strong links with the LVF in County Armagh through Johnny Adair's self-acknowledged 'friendship' with their leaders — decided it was payback time for twenty-nine-year-old Rockett, the LVF bonds were cut.

'He was delivered up like a Christmas turkey for the slaughter,' one loyalist source said afterwards. Rockett, a hardened, recidivist criminal, thought he was safe going back to his old haunts in the North of the city, close to the massive loyalist hot-bed Rathcoole housing estate. But on the fateful Sunday of 18 December, he went on a drinking binge. He was first in a drinking club close to Rathcoole. When he left, 'roaring and yelling' according to some eyewitnesses, he had to be helped down the stairs. However, whether by taxi — or whether some people were 'waiting for' him outside the club — he was taken on to a pub, also in North Belfast. It was from there, probably drunk out of his mind and at least partially impervious to pain and to what was happening to him, that he was bundled into a car and taken to another loyalist hot-bed, Ballysillan, perched at the bottom of the brooding hills that ring that part of the city.

And it was on wasteground in the heart of a housing estate there that two Mafia-style touches heralded the end of William James Rockett's short life. One was the banknotes. The other, unlike Geordie Legge's murder, was that Rockett was despatched from this life with just a solitary, single bullet to the head.

Rockett had been no stranger to trouble: although never of the kind that merited capital punishment. And certainly not by a gang of gun-wielding hoods. By the Sunday after his shooting, I had obtained a supposedly 'confidential' record of Rockett's amazing life of crime. We published a summary of it in the paper, frameworking his convictions from 1985 until two years before his death in 1998. There were no less than *eleven* A4-size pages of the criminal record documents. And they listed no less than 112 convictions for a 'wideboy' who started his criminal career at the tender age of just fourteen years of age. It was then, as a teenager, that he first got sucked into the whirlpool of paramilitarism.

He was first fined £50 at Belfast Juvenile Court for causing a bomb hoax. He was back in the same court two years later. Again, it was a paramilitary-style offence — possessing a petrol bomb with intent, for which he got two years' probation. And those two incidents were the precursor of a life of crime that was to see Rockett ratchet up a life when he committed an average of *seven* offences every year. The catalogue of crime included assault, jay-walking on the motorway, theft, shoplifting, burglary, assault on the police, and a string of motoring offences. In December 1991, Rockett was also involved in a joyriding hit-and-run accident. He was later convicted of taking a motor vehicle without the owner's consent, driving while disqualified, having no insurance, failing to stop after someone was injured, failing to remain at the scene, failing to report the accident, and careless driving. He got four months in prison and was fined £350. Rockett had more — much more — than that stuffed into his pockets when his body was discovered on the Monday morning before Christmas 2000. And he had no convictions for drugs. But then, he didn't start dabbling in those until he went on the run into the ranks of the Portadown LVF. As it was, and as his police record shows, he didn't have a handsome life. But in the end, he had an even uglier death ...

So, too, did one of the drugs 'Godfathers' biggest 'backroom boys'. He was Kieran Smyth, from South Armagh, an allegedly respectable businessman who used the cover of a haulage firm based in the Republic to mask his huge criminal activities. Behind the scenes, the thirty-nine-year-old was a key gangland player in the smuggling of drugs — and guns, and cigarettes — across *seven* countries.

It was reckoned he was the *biggest* money-launderer Ireland had seen since Paddy 'The Fixer' Farrell, the Newry drugs boss supposedly murdered by his mistress in 1997. Paul Williams, the *Sunday World's* award-winning Chief Crime Correspondent in Dublin, wrote that Smyth was laundering up to £3 *million* every *month* for crime gangs and paramilitary racketeers.

His body was found, gagged and bound, in a cattle pen off Kilbrew Lane, five miles from Ashbourne in County Meath, at 3.30 p.m. on Friday, 9 February 2001. Like other drugs underworld and paramilitary victims, he had been brutally beaten before being shot. He had been missing for five days, believed kidnapped from his adopted home at Ravensdale, County Louth, just a few miles from where he was born and brought up as a member of a respected medical family in South Armagh.

He had become known in the underworld as a 'Bagman', and was an international crime figure — who had 'laundered at least £30 million for organised crime and terror gangs before his horrific murder'.

Paul Williams wrote: 'Operating a haulage company from his adopted home in Holland, Smyth had become an essential cog in international crime circles, smuggling drugs, guns and cigarettes. He had been targeted by customs and police in seven countries in recent years. The Dutch authorities had issued an international arrest warrant for him but he had absconded back to Ireland after being released on bail.'

Williams recorded how the Garda Fraud Bureau and Dublin's Criminal Assets Bureau uncovered a huge money-laundering operation along the border in 1999. The official reckoning was that £100 million could have been 'washed' in that single, but huge, scam. And they believe that Smyth's 'wash' in that could have been over a third of the total involved — up to £36 million.

Just weeks before his murder, Smyth had been arrested and questioned. The Dublin authorities probing Smyth's criminal connections froze over £100,000 of his cash. He was due to be questioned again before a file was to be sent to the Director of Public Prosecutions in Dublin. And, as Paul Williams wrote, there could have been 'Godfathers' — either professional, or paramilitary — who feared that Smyth may have turned tout, and scuppered them all.

In Williams's report of Sunday 11 February — six days after Smyth disappeared, and two days after his body was found — he speculated: 'The main theory for the murder is that either a criminal or paramilitary "Godfather" considered him a threat to their ongoing racketeering. He was facing potentially serious charges and could have offered to spill the beans in return for immunity.' He quoted a senior police source as saying: 'This man was involved up to his neck in a serious and highly organised international crime syndicate. He was effectively a very powerful "Bagman" who knew all the big secrets.'

Paul Williams pinpointed another possible theory — that the big-time 'Bagman' had double-crossed one of his powerful associates or owed money.

And there were paramilitary overtones in the Smyth case, too. Williams's post-murder report says: 'Smyth had been doing business and was involved with the Provos, the INLA, and the Real IRA, who between them control all forms of racketeering in the border area.' The RUC had already built up a comprehensive file on his activities. Major drugs barons could not operate in the border area without giving the paramilitaries huge pay-offs (a sinister syndrome covered elsewhere in this book). Paul Williams noted: 'Late last year, four of his lorries were burnt out in an arson attack which detectives now believe could have been a warning ... In December 1998 Gardaí seized £8 million of hash and a large consignment of guns at Castleblayney, County Monaghan. Kieran Smyth's truck was used to smuggle the consignment ...'

Paul also wrote: 'Smyth subsequently successfully claimed back the truck — which was again seized with a shipment of Ecstasy at the port of Calais a month later!' He added: 'At least seven of his trucks have been stopped while carrying contraband in a number of European countries in the past year.' So the wealthy criminal known as 'The Bagman' may have been about to be 'bagged' himself — not only in Ireland, but on the Continent too.

In the end, however, just like Legge, Rockett, Porter, 'Speedy' Fegan, Brendan Campbell, Paddy 'The Fixer' Farrell, 'Big Edd' McCoy and a virtual battalion of drugs dealers murdered in the North before Kieran Smyth — the 'Bagman's' body ended up in a body bag.

That is not to gloat over their demise. It is merely to point out that all were eventually dundered after being involved in the evil drugs trade.

20

The Drugs Buster

'He is undoubtedly one of the best officers the RUC has ever produced. He devoted his life to the police, and to the community. His contribution was immense. My fervent hope is that when the new police service for Northern Ireland is completed, somewhere along the line, someone of the calibre of Kevin Benedict Sheehy will emerge to distinguish its ranks in the same way that 'KB' has honoured, and distinguished, the ranks of the old police service.'

The words were those of another legendary Ulster policeman, Assistant Chief Constable Eric Anderson, the man charged on the RUC side with bringing the infamous Omagh bombers to justice. The Real IRA bomb in Omagh on 15 August 1998 killed twenty-nine men, women and children and two unborn babies, and left scores of other people maimed and injured. One was blinded, others horrifically burned. Top anti-terror detective Mr Anderson had put away many Ulster subversives on both sides — not least the loyalist 'Trick or Treat' killer gang led by UFF gunman Torrens Knight who burst into a public house in the tiny County Derry village of Greysteel one Halloween night and 'sprayed' the pub with a hail of murderous gunfire. And when Omagh erupted, literally, Anderson went in to share with his counterparts in the Garda Síochána the task of finding the ghouls responsible for the single biggest atrocity in the history of the Troubles.

Both teams of detectives, on both sides of the border, now believe they know the identity of the bombers. But knowing the heartless terrorists, and being able to prove their guilt in court, are two entirely different things. Only one man has appeared in court, in Dublin, on an Omagh bombing charge.

When it came to hand-picking his Omagh investigative team, ACC Anderson looked in one direction first: his old friend, colleague and comrade in the front line defence against terrorism, Kevin Sheehy. At that stage, Superintendent Sheehy was working in the RUC Press Office at Knock headquarters. Anderson needed someone to handle the enormous worldwide Press interest in the Omagh investigation.

Mr. Anderson paid his glowing tribute at Kevin Sheehy's recent leaving 'do' from the RUC: the leaving 'do' of a policeman who, during his career, had been honoured by receiving a medal from the Queen at Buckingham Palace. Not bad, as he would say himself, for a 'wee lad' from Queen Street in the heart of the Belfast docklands. Sheehy, like Eric Anderson himself, had decided to take the leaving package frameworked by the Patten Report reforms after many years of service.

One of Kevin Sheehy's most outstanding contributions to the police service, and to the community in Northern Ireland, was when he headed up the RUC's Drugs Squad based at the Antrim Road barracks in North Belfast. He built a team around him who jailed many drugs dealers, and forced more into exile. And, as the following interview shows, the man who charted Ulster's drugs explosion from the start is now fearful for the future, predicting a new 'terror war' waged by drugs gangs. He calls, significantly, for an all-Ireland Drugs Squad to be set up, and warns that, in his view, organised crime will move deeper into the drugs 'Godfather' scene and make the evil trade Ulster's, and Ireland's, Public Enemy Number One.

This is what Kevin Sheehy, Ulster's best-known 'Drugs Buster', says:

Question: When did this whole drugs problem explode in Northern Ireland: was it after the paramilitaries decided to lift their taboo, their ban, on it?

Answer: No, it was actually before that. I would say it was about eight years ago. I think the Provos and every other paramilitary organisation started to look at sources of finance, bearing in mind that the anti-racketeering squad in the RUC was set up in 1982. The squad's function was to identify any source of finance by any paramilitary organisation and make recommendations to government, and government have very successfully brought in legislation, for instance, in relation to registering taxis, insurance for taxis, running night clubs properly, pubs properly, and they were clamping down on counterfeit goods.

So every time the paramilitaries got involved in a financial scam — the building industry is probably the best example — they would tighten up the whole system of accountability. In the 1980s, and right up to 1987/88, there is no doubt about it, builders were writing one or two per cent into contracts to allow for security. But they knew in their hearts that what they were doing was giving up to two per cent of almost every major housing contract to paramilitary organisations.

And we had this terrible situation on the Shankill for instance, where you had Catholic workmen working there, the Provos were in charge of the (workmen's) tax exemption certificates, and the Provos had a working arrangement with the UVF and UDA that the Catholics could work there, and the Prod paramilitaries had a deal whereby they did all the security. And it was the same of course, vice versa, on the Falls. Even when they were road building, every time it went through a Catholic or Protestant area, to the inch, it had to be negotiated with the dominant paramilitary organisation that featured in that specific area.

So the organisations were all working together. There was this background that these organisations were all quite happy to work together, in criminality, and allow things to happen, and bury their old 'war' differences, to make money.

Question: So, were the paramilitaries in from the start of this drugs revolution in Northern Ireland?

Answer: Probably. There was a major difference. The Provos knew that this peace process was coming, and they knew that image was all-important, particularly with the Americans.

They knew what the Americans were like with drugs. So the Provos were very, very clear that their activists weren't going to be allowed to be involved in drugs trafficking. Instead they engaged, or allowed, non-members to be drugs traffickers in West Belfast, Derry, Newry and so on and they agreed to take a percentage of the profits.

The Protestant paramilitaries, UVF, UDA in particular, didn't have so many concerns about image. And they had a long tradition going right back to Jimmy Craig and people like that, that they were always involved in gangsterism.

So they were always trying to make money, and the original arrangement was that for every £5 these people would get, the organisation would get four, and the likes of Jimmy Craig and Billy Quee would get £1. But they very, very subtly turned it round the other way so that they got £4 and the organisation got one. So, as you can imagine, those people are now dead. Billy Quee was allegedly shot by the Provos. But there has always been collusion [between paramilitaries] to eliminate people.

Question: While the Provos were taking money through the back door on drugs, then, for public image, and for the Irish/American image, they were prepared to shoot people dead with the DAAD organisation, and in instances like the 'Night of the Long Guns'?

Answer: Well, you can imagine a top Provo just out of jail, after doing eighteen years for a bombing, caught with heroin or cocaine, or even Ecstasy or cannabis in West Belfast. The Catholic church would come after him, educationalists would come after him, parents would come after him. If you think back to Hugh Brady, he was a Sinn Féin councillor in Derry, had been an activist since the 1970s on behalf of the organisation, he was caught with a moderately small amount of cannabis. His life was made a misery — he was ostracised by the whole organisation. Not because he was caught with a wee bit of cannabis. But because he damaged the image of the organisation at a crucial time when Sinn Féin and the IRA were trying to make themselves credible negotiators in America, to the international audience, and also here.

So their policy has always been that they oversee major drugs trafficking on an international basis, millions of pounds worth, but that their people who have done time in jail are still not, officially, allowed to be involved in that.

Question: So why would the Provos then go for the 'independents' — Mickey Mooney, Speedy Fegan, Brendan Campbell, more recently, Edd McCoy? Because they refused to play ball with the Provos?

Answer: Yes, it's not only that these people are involved in drugs, but these people become cult figures. The likes of Speedy Fegan in Newry spurned and made fun and poked fun at the Provos, and mixed with the itinerants there — all hard men. So while he was driving about in a big fancy car, getting involved in pony trap races for £25,000 at a time, people were saying to the local Provos: 'What are you doing about this wee bastard?' And at some stage then the Provos, to save their own face in the area, had to take action.

The same happened with Brendan Campbell. If you look at all these people, they were all 'hard men' — Brendan Campbell, Edd McCoy, and so on. Brendan Campbell used to drive a top-of-the-range BMW and drive up and down the Falls Road, literally sticking it up the Provos. The individuals that weren't concerned about the Provos, like those we've just mentioned, all had to be eliminated, because they refused to curtail their drugs dealing activities. Or, more importantly, refused to make substantial donations to the Provos.

Now, the Provos are hated among young people who take drugs in this country. And all these guys became cult figures. There are numerous occasions — it's documented — where Provos came into clubs, socialising, and suddenly saw the likes of Edd McCoy, and would try to intimidate him, and McCoy would just get up and blatter them. So all these individuals became cult figures for the young people who hate the Provos. All these kids want to do is take drugs and have a good time. These guys epitomised that lifestyle. And that was the main reason that the Provos eliminated them.

Now, more and more young people are leaving the clubs in West Belfast to go and socialise in the city centre. And that's why, in all these Provo clubs in West Belfast and all over the country, you now have raves, and if you have raves, you have drugs. The Provos know that. To get these kids back into their premises, they had to eliminate the cult figures, so that they could run raves. But they try to present it as a 'social service' to the parents in areas where they have an influence.

Question: So the Provos, in essence, were allowing drugs dealers to operate under 'licence'. But then, on the loyalist side, organisations like the UDA/UFF became big-time operators themselves?

Answer: Yes ... and there's always this history that the Prod paramilitaries are never as well organised or as disciplined as the Provos or any republican organisation: that has always been the case. So what you had was suddenly all this money was coming in, and the Prod organisations couldn't agree with each other. It was easier for them to agree with the Provos. The Provos could produce a business plan (like on the building sites), work out the percentages each crowd would get, and who was allowed to operate. Prod organisations could never do that. So they got greedy, and then suddenly you had this big tension between the UVF and the UFF/UDA in relation to drugs dealing.

And then you had great men like David Ervine who came in with Billy Hutchinson [both Progressive Unionist Party] and tried to stop drugs dealing. And all of a sudden there's horrendous tension — not only between the UFF and the UVF on the Shankill, but among certain elements of the UVF/Red Hand Commando as well, who are into drugs in Bangor, Rathcoole, Newtownabbey. They are saying to the Shankill Road command of the UVF: 'Well, if you're going to put drugs dealing to us, you'd better bring your guns to do it.' So you had this horrendous tension within the UVF as well.

Now, the UFF in a sense were the last to come into the game. But once Johnny Adair started this killing campaign, one of the things he did to make himself very popular was to give his operators what they wanted. They wanted women, they wanted fancy clothes, they wanted fancy lifestyles, they wanted to go to Rangers matches, they wanted drugs — so Johnny authorised this. So any time they did a hit, in his terms 'good work', they had all the cannabis and all the Ecstasy they wanted. But it was mainly the Ecstasy for the raves and the image and the sex and so on ...

Question: Would the killers have been on drugs when they committed some of the atrocities? Would they have bumped E tabs into themselves to get pumped up to go and shoot up a bar, for instance?

Answer: Well, there was an attack on the Boundary Bar [in Belfast] one Saturday afternoon, and it was suggested that the people who did that were on Es. They actually admitted it ... they were on Es. But they knew that the clothes they were wearing would have to be destroyed, and that Johnny's team would supply them with new gear, and that they would have all the drugs they wanted.

Question: So it came from being a reward for terrorism, and developed to the point where a main organisation — like the UFF, for instance, on the Lower Shankill — moved into the drugs scene big-time and were actually supplying a wider circle than just their own people?

Answer: Well, I'm quite certain in my mind now that when big shipments come into Northern Ireland, they are always a percentage of what comes into Britain — maybe representing ten or 15 per cent of a huge shipment coming into Britain. There are people supplying both Catholic and Protestant areas in Northern Ireland now, and there is no doubt in my mind that it's all being done with the agreement and compliance of paramilitary organisations on both sides.

Question: The huge hauls that were captured, particularly during your time, but not only during your time in the Drugs Squad, like a quarter of a million pounds' worth of drugs, half a million pounds' worth, how do they take hits like that and then still get the money to be able to bring in more drugs?

Answer: That's what I'm talking about when I specify this ten or 15 per cent. What they would do is team up with a crowd in, say, Liverpool, where all the money from any source ...

Question: From Dublin as well?

Answer: Yes, I was going to say that ... North and South. If there's a big order going to be placed in Spain for cannabis, or Holland or Belgium for Ecstasy, the word goes out. All the finance travels from Southern Ireland, and from anybody from Northern Ireland who wants in on this.

Question: And it's a rollover factor: the more they sell, the more they can bring in?

Answer: Yes. But if you're going to get involved in the British scene, you have to pay your money on time, no fiddling about, it has to be in Liverpool or wherever on a certain date, so that this can go into the main coffers. And then what you're relying on is that, by getting involved like that on a regular and sustained basis, where the supplier and the buyer trust each other, you get good quality stuff.

So if you're dealing on a frequent basis — say, it takes you six months to get £100,000 together — and you go to see someone in London, he's going to rip you off. But if there's a big shipment coming into Liverpool, and you're there with £80,000 on a regular basis, and they know you're a good customer, you're made.

Question: Who are these suppliers in the likes of Liverpool?

Answer: There would be a big Irish connection from the Republic — Liverpool Irish. But the main element is English, English gangsters. Liverpool is a huge centre ... for me, it is probably the main danger to the whole of Ireland for drugs trafficking. So there's that big central-isation. There is an Irish connection there. But the core would be Liverpudlians themselves. But they would have major criminal contacts with the likes of London, Glasgow, Manchester, in particular.

Question: What about the Irish connection then, across the border? 'Godfathers' like Paddy Farrell, who was shot dead, allegedly by his mistress — I don't think too many people believe that theory, actually. But Paddy Farrell, sitting down in Newry, he would have acted as a conduit between the North and South on big drugs deals?

Answer: Well, Paddy Farrell's responsibility would have been as the 'purse mixer', or 'fixer', on the finance going over to Liverpool. He would be the person who would work out with the big Dublin men: 'Right, how much do we need for the whole of Ireland?' Northern Ireland was never considered in isolation.

Take the likes of Speedy Fegan. In a big week, once one of these big consignments came into Liverpool, Farrell would have organised all the finance, and then the percentage split based on that. So, say, 500 kilos (of cannabis) would come into Dublin. Farrell would take maybe 200 kilos to Cork. Say, 100 kilos to Limerick. And then 100 kilos up North and into the hands of the likes of Fegan. And then the Dubs themselves may also have put another 100 or 200 kilos into Dublin.

Question: Would 'The General', Martin Cahill, have been involved with that? Because there are suggestions that the likes of loyalist terrorist Billy Wright, whenever he was around, did business with Martin Cahill.

Answer: Yes ... the police and the authorities down in Dublin have been actually brilliant in identifying the main drugs traffickers. And the newspapers down there — particularly the likes of the *Sunday World* — have done big hits in terms of identifying the main drugs 'Godfathers'.

They have high-profiled them — criminals like 'The Penguin' and so on.

All of those drugs barons, their responsibility would be to decide how much their gang needed, and then work through the likes of 'The General', or 'The Penguin', or John Gilligan, or Paddy Farrell.

So what you would have is, say, four big gangs in Dublin, Farrell straddling the border, various groupings up here, all getting all this money together and all to be taken over safely by couriers. And this is where Fegan would come in. Once that stuff came into Dublin, into the big Gilligan warehouse, Fegan would be told: 'Right, you and your team are doing Cork, Limerick, Newry, Belfast and Ballymena once this comes in.' He would get his order. It was rumoured that Fegan was maybe only getting £100 for delivering a kilo. And yet we all know that he ran pony-trotting races where he could place bets of £25,000.

So it shows you the volume of stuff that was coming in when Farrell was alive, and Fegan was alive, and when another boy — still alive — was based in Ulster (he's since moved base). He was bringing in 100 kilos a time. And he was doing that on a very, very regular basis. And I think the last time one of his hauls was seized, there was something like ninety kilos of cannabis in it.

Question: So what is the overall picture?

Answer: Northern Ireland is part of the European drugs situation. It's part of the big picture. Any problem you read about Dublin (minus heroin), that's Northern Ireland.

Question: You mentioned heroin. You also mentioned the so-called 'Bible Belt' town of Ballymena. It now has a serious, and growing, heroin problem, with a spiralling number of registered addicts. Heroin is taking hold in Northern Ireland, too, isn't it?

Answer: Yes, I've also said that is the barometer. If you get heroin and cocaine taking a hold, then you've got a very serious problem.

Question: Has it taken hold?

Answer: I think it has taken a major hold in the likes of Ballymena. Ballymena, in spite of its 'Bible Belt' label, is the 'trendy' place to look for it. Unless you look for it, you're not going to find it.

Now, I would think that there's a developing heroin problem in Belfast, and Newry, as we speak. But when you think of it, Newry is only fifty miles away from Dublin, Belfast one hundred miles. So with Dublin's heroin problem, the spread is almost inevitable.

And if you look at the Scottish port of Stranraer, the ferry port just across the Irish Sea, there is apparently a horrendous heroin problem there ... and Stranraer is just twenty-one miles from Northern Ireland. And once that's in, you can never get rid of it.

Question: How serious is the problem now, compared to when you started to tackle it in the Drugs Squad?

Answer: On the sliding scale of one to five when I started, we were at two. I would say we are at four, now.

Question: So how can it be stopped, or even curtailed?

Answer: The RUC have done well, bearing in mind the background of terrorism, but the whole system has become more sophisticated. You tell the story about the drugs dealer wanting a driver to courier drugs in his cement lorry. You can't stop a cement lorry and ask it to dump its load. What you need to do is get the intelligence before the stuff comes in. So what you have to do is identify the financiers, the drugs dealers, the methods of bringing it in, the routes they're using to bring it in. But most of all you have to identify the contacts in Liverpool and London in particular. Northern Ireland and Ireland will not prosper until we identify all of that drugs-supply tapestry.

So, it's time for an all-Ireland Drugs Squad. It's time for the RUC, or the new police service, to have representatives working in England with the National Drugs Intelligence Unit. It's time the police here had representatives working there full-time. And inter-police contacts need to be built up between Ireland and Europe, particularly Amsterdam. Amsterdam and Liverpool have such a horrendous record of drugs imports. Every police force in Britain and in Europe wants work done in Amsterdam. But the Amsterdam police are too busy. But if you have a representative out there, and you're working with them, they'll do more and more work for you. It's the same in Liverpool. We need somebody working there in Liverpool. Every police force in Britain wants the Liverpool police to do work with them.

Question: But you're saying that more resources in any police force — and you're calling for an all-Ireland Drugs Squad — should be poured into that aspect of policing to combat this problem now ...

Answer: Well, I have this suspicion in England, where you get this finite budget, that it is suggested that some chief constables are looking to focus on issues that are most in the newspapers and most in people's minds — traffic accidents, burglaries, domestic violence, street crime, taking and driving away.

The drugs problem is one of those insidious things. It's all underground. Unless you go looking for it, you don't find it. But the problem is, if you've a limited budget, if you go looking for it and you know it's there, you have to do something about it.

Which means resources, expert resources. It's no use just asking policemen on the beat to deal with it. You need specially trained people. You need very sophisticated equipment. You need surveillance. You need surveillance cars. You need top-of-the-range radio communication systems. You need people specifically trained in surveillance, undercover work, handling informants. You need money to pay informants. You need all of those things. And this new police service (for Northern Ireland) needs to address this very substantially.

If they are going to make a public declaration of intent, it will have to be at the stage they start recruiting. When they start to train people for this new police service, then the public will have to look to see the priority they are giving to the drugs problem. Every policeman and policewoman will have to play their part. But that means that at the training stage, the fight against drugs is given a higher priority than in the past for every recruit going through ... and at the other end, that more resources are made available to take on the drugs 'Godfathers'.

Question: Personally, in your time in the Drugs Squad, is there one drugs 'Godfather' that gave you particular pleasure to take on, put away, or perhaps pressurise so much that he left the country?

Answer: Well, there are a number of people. Liam Mooney is one we've managed to drive out of the country.

Speedy Fegan is now dead. He was a top target, in another sense, for the Drugs Squad. Paddy Farrell was a top target in that sense, as well. Paul Daly is dead too.

So the RUC, in fairness to them, like the Garda Siochána, they can actually identify the main drugs dangers to Northern Ireland and Ireland, and that's to their eternal credit. But the main thing for me is that police forces should declare the drugs problem as a major, major priority. Because I believe drugs abuse is going to be one of the biggest social issues facing Northern Ireland — and Ireland, and Britain, and Europe — for the next twenty years.

Question: There is a drive in some quarters to have cannabis legalised. Would you support that, having seen what you have seen, and now knowning what you know after your time in the Drugs Squad?

Answer: The whole issue of legalising cannabis … we've heard this argument from the 1960s. But I don't think many people know that the top-class cannabis that is available today is *twenty* times more powerful than the cannabis that was around in the 1960s. So we need to be very careful here. I have no problem with cannabis being made available for medical research. That stands to reason. If it can help people who are desperately ill with a certain limited number of conditions, that's fine. But anybody who talks about 'soft' and 'hard' drugs — they're talking nonsense. There are people in this country and in England who are addicted to cannabis. As soon as they get out of bed, they need cannabis. Cannabis traces remain in the body tissues for up to thirty days. So if you take two or three cannabis cigarettes a day — that concentration of PHC, which is the main chemical ingredient — it's a huge build-up. And it does affect concentration. And it will affect the ability to learn, to take knowledge, and to retain knowledge.

So, there are a whole lot of issues. But, the main thing I'm saying is that cannabis is far more potent and powerful now than it was. Then, of course, there are all the issues related to cancers. They talk about cigarette tars, but cannabis tars are far more concentrated.

Question: So you wouldn't be in favour of legalising cannabis?

Answer: No.

Question: Finally, if we are to have peace from the terror war in this society — and we now have what is called an 'imperfect peace' — is drugs the biggest danger now facing this society?

Answer: For me, in terms of criminality, drugs would come first, organised crime — racketeering — a close second. But if you are going to look at drugs in Northern Ireland in the future, you are looking at organised crime as well. No longer are you going to get some kid gathering together two thousand pounds, going to England, bringing back E tabs, and making a profit. The drugs trade in future will be organised by ruthless people who are quite happy not only to terrorise, but to brutalise and kill people. We know that has been the case history in this country in the past.

Question: So we're talking about a new 'terror war', revolving around drugs?

Answer: That's my view, yes ...

Epilogue

❖

This book could get me a bullet, or a bomb. That is not said lightly.

It is by no means a cheap attempt to put me anywhere near on a par with Veronica Guerin, or my colleague Martin O'Hagan, both shot dead for their very focused, very thorough, and very professional pursuit of major drugs 'Godfathers' in Dublin and in Ulster.

However, in reporting on drugs barons, I simply do my job, as do the other reporters in the *Sunday World*. But our exposure of the rise and rise of drugs 'Godfathers' in Ulster has brought its share of threats and, in the case of the firebombing of our office, direct action from ruthless, greedy and rich criminals who believe they can live beyond the law, and get away with it. In a lot of cases, they haven't. They were gunned down by other criminals operating in a 'vigilante' role, like the gunmen and assassins of DAAD. Where that has happened, we have tried to expose those murderers, and what lies behind them, as well.

As I have said elsewhere in this book, in the same way that we oppose all forms of terrorism in our society, we also oppose any forms of summary justice (kangaroo courts) or summary maiming or execution (knee-cappings, or murders). The place for criminals, especially those who deal in the evil trade of drugs, is behind bars: pure and simple. That is the ethos on which we work. It is summed up in what I reported earlier in the book when I was confronted by the drugs baron Brendan 'Speedy' Fegan after he was first shot and wounded. When he accused me of getting him the two slugs he was still carrying in his chest, I told him he'd brought that on himself — for poisoning the kids of this country.

And that, in essence, is what this book is about. It is not meant as an academic treatise or a library reference tome. It is not meant as a full documentary of the growing drugs menace in Northern Ireland. Instead, it is meant as a snapshot, a brief drama-documentary almost, of the drugs culture that is threatening to consume, harm and even kill our children.

This drugs culture is coming on the back of a thirty-one-year terror war. The paramilitaries who waged death and destruction are now, in some cases, turning to the drugs trade to preserve their power bases and their penchant for the high life.

The latest published statistics, for the year 2000, chart the real upsurge in drugs. In 1999, just over 163,000 E tabs were seized. In 2000, the quantity of pills soared to 448,015 tablets, over four and a half times the amount of Ecstasy powder seized the previous year.

The amount of opiates seized has skyrocketed in just twelve months, with 464.8 grams being uncovered and confiscated by police. More recently, and outside of the ambit of those police figures, a heroin haul with an estimated street value of £1 million — in one cache alone — was seized in North Belfast. In 1999, the amount of cocaine seized was over *ten* times what it had been the previous year. Cannabis seized has also spiralled dramatically.

The following year, it was over *ten* times that much — 4,923.3 gm, according to the police statistics.

Arrests in 2000, compared with 1991, have gone through the roof: 1,254 suspects nicked, compared to under a third of that number charged or cautioned just eight years previously.

Is it entirely coincidental that the biggest users, those in the eighteen–thirty age bracket — the most formative section of our society in Northern Ireland now — are the people who lived *all* of their lives through the thirty-one-year trauma of the Troubles? I'll leave that one for the psychoanalysts and sociologists to ponder.

The Rev. Eric Smyth, a clergyman and councillor in the city, was Lord Mayor when former US President Bill Clinton visited the city on his famous 'peace mission' at Christmas 1995. He was on the podium with Bill Clinton the night he made the 'your day is over' speech to terrorists in front of a cheering crowd of thousands outside Belfast City Hall.

The veteran councillor, with personal knowledge of the drugs cancer in society (his son was jailed for drugs offences) summed up: 'I look forward to the day when, like President Clinton said to the terrorists in Ulster, I can say to the drugs "Godfathers" – "Your days are over ..."'

In writing this book, and knowing — and having known — many of those drugs dealers, I would like to be able to say I am confident that, some day, that will happen. But I'd be telling you, the reader, a lie, if I did. All I — and hacks, reporters, journalists, call us what you will — can pledge to do is to keep chasing and exposing drugs dealers. Then, maybe they'll go running for the trees. And then, just like one actor said at the recent Screen Actors' Guild awards, maybe, like the monkey, 'the further you climb up the tree, the more you show of your ass.' And if we can drive the drugs 'Godfathers' even a little way up the trees, maybe

we can all work together not only to see more of their asses ...
but to make sure they end up with their asses where they belong.
Behind bars. And out of our kids' — and harm's — way ...

Appendix

J ust before Christmas 2000 the people fighting the drugs scourge in Ulster got an early present. But it wasn't Santa who delivered it. Instead, it was the Department of Health and Social Services. They announced on 8 December 2000 that they were appointing Northern Ireland's very own 'Drugs Czar'. That underlined — as if any underpinning was needed — how serious the problem has become in the Province.

Less than two months later, Jo Daykin walked into the Stormont office at the DHSS HQ designated for the 'Drugs Czar'. Her official title is Drugs Strategy Co-ordinator for Northern Ireland, though when I appeared on a recent TV panel discussion with her, she didn't baulk at the title 'Drugs Czar'.

Little wonder. Thirteen years previously she founded the Dunlewey Substance Advice Centre at a time when substance misuse was an increasing problem in Belfast. That started as a pioneering, community-based project, and has developed into a cutting- and leading-edge agency in the field of addiction. She also became involved in a phalanx of community initiatives, picking up academic qualifications at the University of Ulster on the way. In 1996 she was appointed Chair of the Eastern Drugs Co-ordination Team (EDCT) and Chair of the EDCT Voluntary and Community Forum. And she has been an active member of the Belfast Education and Library Board and the Lisburn Peace and Reconciliation Partnership Board. So the background and experience are certainly there.

So what has the new 'Drugs Czar' to say? Just five weeks into her new post when this interview took place, she gave me her perspective on the problem being perpetuated by Ulster's drugs 'Godfathers'.

Question: Jo, You are, to use tabloidese, Ulster's new 'Drugs Czar'. How serious do you assess the drugs problem to be here?

Answer: I think the drugs problem here is something that we can't be complacent about. I am a great one for hesitating on words about how serious it is because people have different definitions. Can we say that in the early 1990s, when I was in the voluntary and community sector, what Northern Ireland had in those days was problems with alcohol, solvents and prescribed drugs. What we have now is a very clear and visible drugs market, and it is a scene that is growing. And in the truest sense of the word when we are talking about young people and the risk to their lives, it is serious.

Question: A survey was published last week that showed that in the eighteen to thirty-five age group, one in five of those polled said that they had taken drugs or were taking drugs. Twenty per cent having tried drugs — and, the survey also indicated, one in four having taken them more than once — is a big clump of a young adult population to be involved in any way with drugs.

Answer: Yes, it certainly is. And my worry would be how many of those kids were maybe using and experimenting out of peer pressure or curiosity, and how many of those kids will not leave it at that and progress on to other drugs and end up with really serious problems in the future. That is the kind of area that I think people like me — and not just me, because this problem is bigger than any department — really will require all of us working together to deal with it.

The issue that I think needs to be addressed is: 'Yes, look at all those kids trying [drugs], and many of them are going to end up with serious problems if Northern Ireland doesn't get this tragedy ruled out, doesn't get the education programmes rolled out and into the schools.

Question: In terms of the problem, we have seen huge consignments of heroin seized recently — £1 million worth on the Antrim Road in Belfast alone. The RUC said that that was bound for Ballymena, where there is a very high heroin addiction problem at the moment: are the hard drugs biting in?

Answer: Yes, I think they are. Northern Ireland was very lucky for an awful long time not to have had a drugs scene or drugs problem to begin with, and it was surrounded by countries that had, like down South and across the water in the UK. But when we did get a drugs problem, we had a hungry market here.

It is my opinion that when drugs reached Northern Ireland they took a hold, they took a grip much quicker than perhaps in a lot of other countries.

We again had a very long time when we didn't have a heroin problem and there was a little comfort in that. But we can't say that in Northern Ireland anymore. Heroin is in Northern Ireland and like all the other drugs it is increasing and spreading. Now, it has got to be kept in context.

We're still seeing today, and we're still able to say that our heroin problem is not as bad as the UK and it is not as bad as Dublin. But yes, heroin is in Northern Ireland, people are using heroin, and the number of people using heroin is increasing.

Question: You see all kinds of statistics bandied about. Are there any hard statistics, does anybody know what the heroin abuse statistics are here?

Answer: I feel the answer to that, in honesty, is probably no. I think some of the things that you have to remember in terms of research in relation to illicit drugs is that you are researching something that, by its very nature, is illegal. So the quality of the information that you are going to get has to be questioned. That is not to say that we don't need research. I don't want you to hear that, we do need research and we need it very desperately. But we have to be mindful when we are quoting all these figures of what we are actually talking about. In terms of heroin, no, I am not aware of a really good, recent up-to-date, qualitative piece of research that could say there are 'X' amount of people using heroin in Northern Ireland.

There are all sorts of gauges: some of them are good, and some are bad, and there is all sorts of ad hoc information. But there is nothing hard. Why we know that it is a problem in Northern Ireland and why we know it is a problem in specific areas like Ballymena, for example, and North Down, is its visibility. What we are getting is heroin use increasing and it is becoming more and more visible.

Now, part of the Drugs Strategy for Northern Ireland sets out a number of aims with a number of objectives attached to each aim, and one of the things that we need to do and what we are doing at the minute is to establish base lines for the kind of questions that you have just asked me — base lines that will tell us as best as we will ever know what the level of heroin use is out there: how many kids are using Ecstasy, how many kids are presenting for treatment, what is the typical age when they begin to experiment. These are the kinds of questions that we need answers to.

Question: Do you believe, Jo, when it comes to heroin use — and this argument comes up with parliamentarians and politicians — that the use of soft drugs leads on to the use of narcotics like heroin? And if that is the case, what can you do as the 'Drugs Czar' for Northern Ireland to stop bouncers on club doors from selling E tabs to young people going into clubs, or pubs, or whatever?

Answer: Well, the first part of your question was about soft drugs leading onto hard. I think again that this is one of those areas where there is a two-sided answer. In my experience, and not just as Drugs Strategy Coordinator, but also in the voluntary and community sector, I have very rarely met anybody that was using and having addiction problems with hard drugs who didn't start with cannabis. Equally though, it must be said, not everybody who smokes cannabis goes onto harder drugs. So it's one of those curious scenarios where I don't think you can use bland statements like 'anyone who uses cannabis ends up on heroin'. That's simply not the truth. But it is certainly the gateway drug for a certain element of people. And from that point of view, and for a whole lot of other reasons, it is not my opinion that cannabis or any of the other so-called 'soft' drugs should be legalised.

I think we get into arguments that we mix up. For instance, in terms of cannabis I will often hear people saying that cannabis should be legalised because it is really good for MS sufferers. My response to that is, if the medical profession come along and say to us that they have concrete evidence that cannabis can provide something to people who are sick, then great, let's have it available on prescription and let's make it available to people like that. My own mother, when she was dying, got heroin to make her passing easier. That is not to say I want those kinds of things socially available. There are two arguments.

Question: How do you stop them being socially available — cannabis, E tabs, or whatever? Is that purely a job for the police, or is it part of your education programme to teach kids to make the decision for themselves not to take these things, and not to buy them?

Answer: I think it's both. Throughout the whole drugs field, if you like, you always have the two arguments of supply and demand. I think that those are factors that have to be focused on and that you have to work with ...

In terms of the actual suppliers, that is by and large a police matter, and they get on with it, and I think that they get on with it very well. But in terms of demand, I think that is where the Drugs Strategy and people like me need to focus. We have to look and not just rely on the drugs being taken off the streets. I think we have to educate our young people about drugs, but not simply by 'this is an E tab and it's bad for you'. We have to take a much more holistic approach in my opinion. If you look at any young person who uses drugs and who then continues to use drugs to the point where problems occur, very often you will discover that there are other underlying factors. It might be low self-esteem, it might be a death in the family they haven't been able to cope with — whatever — the range is wide and varied.

But usually what they can often find is that the drugs keep them out of the reality of life that they can't cope with. It is very important if we want to stop kids getting into drugs, if we want them to make healthier choices about themselves, that we bring them to a place where they believe in themselves, bring them to a place where they know their own self-worth, where they know their own importance and their own uniqueness, and where they are standing saying: 'I, Joe Bloggs, at the ripe old age of thirteen, am a very important part of society and I have a lot to contribute when I get older.'

Now, you don't do that in five minutes, and you certainly don't do it with a thirteen-year-old in five minutes, even when you have them. It's a very strange time, adolescence, at the best of times — without kids having their heads messed up with drugs on top of it.

Question: This is a personal question. If you had a sixteen-year-old boy or girl, and you discovered E tabs or dope or blow in their pockets, what would you say to them?

Answer: Yes, I have teenagers, a sixteen-year-old, as it happens, and it is very interesting because a lot of people in the field have this conversation and I think we are great ones for saying to parents 'don't do that' and 'don't go over the top' and 'you must keep the communication lines open' and all the rest, and I really believe that that is what needs to happen. Time and time again we have had — again I am going back to my past life and experience in the voluntary community sector— kids coming through my door, trailed in by their mothers because there was a bit of dope or an E tab found. And the whole situation has been allowed to escalate out of control and really become like a red rag to the kid because of the parent's reaction.

When you sit them down and you get the communication lines open and you start to get into the feelings and the kid begins to realise the mother's fear and what's behind their reaction and so on, then you find there is a greater chance of the kids knocking it on the head, and kids knocking it on the head not simply because their parents are demanding that they do.

So, my response to my own kids would be very much in and around probably having a ballistic attack — on my own, against myself! — in a room well away from them, and then coming out much calmer and going down the road of what drugs they had, why they had it, how long they have been taking it, what pleasure are they getting out of it, why do they did they feel a need to feel that way? Checking it out, my big focus would be their motivation. I would be feeling much more relieved as a parent if my kid said: 'Well, I took it because everybody else was' than if they said: 'I took it because I was bored' or 'I took it because it makes me feel good about myself'.

Question: That's exactly it. How do you counter that? Your kids are going out and going to clubs and pubs and they say to you: 'I took it because everybody else is, and it is available'. And, let's face it, it is available in a lot of places. How do you respond to that?

Answer: I think that this is the hardest bit about drugs. I think you have to respond to drugs just like most other things that kids do because of peer pressure, because everybody else is doing it. You have to start working with your kid and replacing their self-esteem, and their self-belief, and their self-worth. I, like any parent, have had kids come in and I have caught them smoking. I have had my own kids come in at the age of fourteen and fifteen and they were out of their heads with alcohol because their mates were drinking.

I have had to sit them down and go through that whole process with them of finding self-worth and self-esteem and what is right for them ... very often the thing that I also hang on to, and I have had this experience with my own kids as well as dealing with other people's kids. Very often when a young person does something like that, be it drink or be it drugs, you actually find, when the communication channel is open, that they didn't actually enjoy it and they didn't like it and they knew they were doing something they shouldn't have been doing and the whole guilt element got in the way of their enjoyment.

And there's an element of relief in the young person's part when it does come out and Mummy and Daddy aren't going ballistic, but are coming from a place of: 'OK, it's happened. But how can we make sure it doesn't happen again?' And giving them answers for young people, and for their friends.

One of the things that I would do a lot with my kids is role play. That sounds very dramatic. But if my kids were going to a place where there is a chance that something would happen, then I would say (in the role play of being a drugs dealer): 'OK, I'm offering you this. What are you going to say to me?' And I actually would get my kids to go through with me how they would protect themselves.

So it's a combination. But it's still very much about communication. It's about getting to the kid's place, and understanding why they did it, and then bringing the kid along with you as to why they shouldn't.

Question. Jo, you're talking now about kids who may feel bad or whose parents may catch them on. But what about a kid or a teenager who says to you: 'I take it because it makes me feel good'?

Answer. What I would say to parents in that situation is: Don't feel that you're on your own. Take a very deep breath and get your child and yourself down to the nearest centre that offers counselling and advice. Not just for the young person, but indeed for parents. I think parents far too often feel isolated, feel fearful, feel judged that their kids are taking drugs. They try to handle it their own way, and on their own. And by the time they realise they cannot, and it's bigger than them, there's a lot more damage done. And I would simply say to parents: 'If you can't cope and your kid can't cope — get help. It's out there. And don't be afraid to ask for it.'

Question: Bottom line, Jo, is this. This book will reflect my experiences as a hack over thirty-two years, seeing the drugs problem implode in Northern Ireland. The book is being written as a warning to parents. It's going to reflect that there are evil bastards out there who are only interested in gelt, and the high life, and pushing drugs to kids.

You haven't been in this job long — about a month — but from your previous experience are you optimistic or pessimistic about how this whole scenario can be handled?

Answer: I said at the beginning of the interview, and I'll say it again: the drugs situation in Northern Ireland is bigger than me and you. It is going to take all of us to work together, and by working together we are not going to eradicate drugs in Northern Ireland. You and I will never see a drugs-free Northern Ireland again. We have to be terribly realistic and we have to acknowledge that. Anybody thinking different, they're living in cloud cuckoo land.

But by working together and by getting together, what we can see is a beginning in turning the drugs situation around. The kids that are looking at drugs at around the age of eleven or twelve are usually doing it out of curiosity or experimentation. We can bring a lot of kids out of that experimenting stage before any problems start. And we can raise the number of kids who just don't even bother getting into the whole experimentation in the first place.

We can ensure that those kids who do get into bother have proper facilities out there. And we can ensure, and I think this is the biggest bit of work, that the generation coming up, that my nineteen-month-old grandchild will be sitting at eight, nine and ten believing in himself, whereas many kids of that age today maybe don't. I think the adults in our society, the teachers, the parents and the churches have got to realise that personal development is not just a 'cool' thing to say. It's not just Americanised 'new thinking'. It happens to be about helping human beings develop to their full potential.

This is something that I think we haven't done in Northern Ireland completely. So we talk about drugs. But I want to go back, and if you want to call this approach wishy-washy, call it wishy-washy — but for me the real work is beginning with our toddlers today. And it's not about teaching them about Ecstasy and LSD and cannabis and how dangerous they are. It's about teaching them, the kids, how important they are, as individuals. That is where the real work has to be done.

Question: OK, so let's go back to the original question: optimistic, or pessimistic?

Answer: Optimistic.